Nearshore Marketing

NEARSHORE MARKETING

How Nearshore Providers Can Leverage Digital Marketing to Enter the U.S. Market

Fernando A Labastida

Lab Dav Publishing
Round Rock, Texas

DEDICATION

I dedicate this book to the loving memory of my father Fernando Labastida, who passed away right after I got the first proof of this book. He was the most wonderful person in the world. A true intellectual giant. He personified international relations as a top United Nations functionary and a person driven by high ideals. This book is for you papa.

CONTENTS

Advance Praise for Nearshore Marketing   ix

Preface   xi
     Fernando A. Labastida

Introduction – The Nearshore Marketing Model   1

1. How to Position Your Service In The U.S. Market   29

2. Your Number one Marketing Tool   42

3. How to Establish Authority to Make Selling Easy   52

4. The Right Way to Build Your Website   65

5. How to Drive Traffic to Your Website   79

6. Selling 2.0: How to Reach The Right Customers   90

7. How to Close More Sales With the Escalation Model   107

8. Conclusion   119

About the Author   125

ADVANCE PRAISE FOR NEARSHORE MARKETING

"Fernando Labastida showcases his hands-on sales & marketing expertise into a comprehensive guide… This is a terrific and practical handbook full of actionable advice, touching on many areas pertinent in the B2B marketing and highly recommended for any executive that wants to sell Nearshore services in the U.S. market."

– Marcelo Gomes de Costa, CMO, NEORIS

"The Nearshore Marketing Book is an outstanding read, providing rich detail and instructions for Nearshore companies trying to improve their business development models in North America and globally. The section on establishing authority and leveraging content to build distinction in the marketplace is especially valuable. I hope more Nearshore companies follow this very sound guidance!"

– Kirk Laughlin, Managing Editor, Nearshore Americas

"The keys to success are always in the details, and if you're a business from Mexico, Central or South America, trying to sell to the U.S. IT market, those details can be found in Nearshore Marketing. To tell you that this book teaches you how to succeed in the U.S. would do it a huge disservice. What you have here is the blueprint for success–from someone who has experience breaking through the clutter and getting heard. If you're trying to sell nearshore services to the U.S., read this book now!"

– Kathryn Aragon, Content Strategist & Consultant, Author of The Business Blog Handbook

There's good news and bad news when you are offering outsourced services to the North American market. The bad news is there are many companies like yours trying to do the same. The good news is the vast majority of them are doing a lousy job by spamming, cold calling and ultimately delivering a message all about them that does not build a relationship of trust with their prospects. You can certainly do better than them! The GREAT news is that Fernando Labastida and his Nearshore Marketing Book gives you the concrete advice and guidance you need to stand out from your competitors around the world. Implement Fernando's ideas and you will gain many happy clients.

– Steve Mezak, CEO, Accelerance, Author of Software without Borders and Outsource or Else!

PREFACE

Fernando A. Labastida

In January of 2009 I was laid off from my corporate sales job in software sales. I had been working in the startup software space for about 15 years, and had been through my fair share of ups and downs, from fast growing venture funded startups, to IPOs, to layoffs and more layoffs.

In 2007 I discovered blogging. I started to enhance my sales process by blogging about issues that were of concern to my customers. I was selling data integration software, so I started blogging about how data integration could benefit businesses by achieving seamless, automated connections between disparate databases, applications, and business partners.

I think I was doing too much blogging and not enough selling. So, when the 2008-2009 financial crisis hit, my sales pipeline vanished almost overnight and I became a statistic.

I had never been happier! I was finally free to pave my own path and become my own boss. But, I didn't know what to do. I talked to several people, including my good friend, Gerardo Dada, who, at the time, was a rising star at Microsoft. He told me about this new thing called *nearshore outsourcing*. Outsourcers from Latin America, which were located close to the United States in the same time zones, and were selling their services to American companies, were considered *nearshore* instead of *off shore*.

I got really excited about this. As a completely a bi-lingual English/Spanish speaker, I had always gravitated towards doing business in Latin America. I was always making connections between U.S. companies and companies from Latin America, and I loved traveling.

The nearshore phenomenon was the perfect market for me to become involved with. I decided to become a marketing consultant helping Latin American technology outsourcers enter the U.S. market by using modern marketing methods, like content marketing, social media, email, and other digital strategies.

I started a blog, *Latin IT Marketing* (http://latinitmarketing.com), and began sharing my marketing and sales knowledge, as well as what I was learning about content marketing and social media, in Spanish. I wrote my blog posts for software development companies and other outsourcers to teach them how to market and sell their services in the United States.

I also became a guest blogger at Nearshore Americas, providing tips and how-to's for Latin American outsourcers.

My blogging attracted the attention of folks involved in the nearshore outsourcing space, from government officials to CEOs of outsourcing firms in Argentina, Costa Rica, Panama, and Mexico.

This book is the result of everything I've learned, experienced, seen, and become passionate about: helping the growing number of Latin American outsourcers penetrate the U.S. market using modern marketing methodologies.

I couldn't have written it without the help and valuable support of so many people, including:

Kathryn Aragon, content marketing expert, thought leader and author, who through her selfless and patient coaching and mentoring helped guide me through this whole process.

Karla Gomez, my designer, who patiently cranked out one version after another of different book covers, until I got past my fickle self and chose the final design.

And to Mónica Jiménez who encouraged me to write the book, and kept me focused on the one goal...thank you so much for your support.

And all the following people who've been so helpful throughout this process:Jorge Zavala, Gerardo Dada, Steve Mezak, Kirk Laughlin, Mauricio Duran, Cesar D'Onofrio, Alex Camino, Marcelo Costa, Paula Amador, Karen Liedl, Jose Omar Mosco, Jeffrey Eisenberg, Bryan Eisenberg, Brian Massey, Peep Laja, José Gonzalez, Guillermo Gonzalez King, and Omari Broussard.

INTRODUCTION – THE NEARSHORE MARKETING MODEL

"Any organization in which marketing is either absent or incidental is not a business and should never run as if it were one." – Peter Drucker, *The Practice of Management*

Can outsourcers from Latin America challenge companies from India to become the dominant providers in the IT and back-office outsourcing market?

Can you, as a company from Mexico, Brazil, Argentina, Colombia, Costa Rica, Dominican Republic, Chile, Uruguay or Peru, become the next Cognizant, TCS, Wipro, or Infosys?

Look at the list of the *Top 10 IT Service Providers of the Year* published by CIO.com. Of the top ten, four are from India and the rest are from the United States. Will there be a day when the list has at least one firm from Latin America? Or maybe two or three?

Will one of those firms be yours?

Nearshore outsourcing – the term used to describe outsourcing to Latin America from the U.S. – has been around for about twenty years. Unfortunately, we still have not seen companies from The Americas become major players on the world stage.

I believe that can change.

To achieve market dominance, I believe you, as a software development, IT management, or business process outsourcing company from Latin America, must take a completely different approach. You need to stop trying to compete like the Indian, Russian, and Filipino companies do, and create a new strategy.

To really achieve breakthrough success, you need to change the rules of the game, and not play by everybody else's rules.

In this book I talk about the secret weapon Latin American companies can use to change the rules of the game and become dominant players in the outsourcing market.

In the following pages you'll discover how you, as an outsourcer from the American continent, can adopt modern marketing methodologies to create a new market for your company and start to drive exponential success selling your services in the U.S. and Canadian markets.

But first, a little background on how we got here.

Nearshore Outsourcing: The New Hope

Since the creation of the term "nearshore outsourcing" by Mexican IT services firm Softtek in the late 1990s, we've seen an explosion of software development companies, IT services firms and BPO providers from Latin America selling their services in the U.S. market.

They're challenging the dominance of the Indian outsourcing juggernaut, and proving that smart, innovative companies from the American continent can make a name for themselves in the most competitive business market in the world.

Names like Softtek, NEORIS, CI&T, Globant, Making Sense, Stefanini and iTexico have blazed trails, capturing market share and proving that you don't have to look to India or Russia to outsource your software development or back office services.

American companies can now outsource their IT, back office operations, and software development to captive data centers, development teams, call centers, and business process outsourcing companies in Latin America in the Caribbean – just south of the largest market in the world!

American companies can actually have real-time conversations with their new providers during normal working hours and not have to stay up late at night to talk to teams in Mumbai or Bangalore.

They can jump on a quick flight to Guadalajara, San José, Costa Rica, or Mexico City, stay a few days meeting their team and touring their facilities, and fly back home in time to spend the weekend with the family.

Nearshore represents the brave new world of outsourcing. It promises to change things forever. It has opened up a new frontier for American companies. We discovered a whole new continent of possibilities in an area we only thought of as a place to enjoy a beach vacation.

As a result, we've seen a big uptick in the formation of software development, IT management, call-center, and BPO companies from Mexico, Argentina, Brazil, Colombia, Costa Rica, Peru and other countries offering their services to the U.S. market. These firms saw the opportunity and started marketing themselves using the selling points created by Softtek.

Despite the existence of hundreds of software and back-office outsourcing providers – from Mexico all the way to Argentina – Latin America, as a destination for outsourcing, has still not captured the public imagination as it should.

The problem with Nearshore is...Nearshore

In a 2013 interview with Nearshore Americas, Deborah Kops of Sourcing Change said, "Outsourcing companies spend very little money on sales, marketing, and branding. Marketing is the front door of any business, but outsourcers aren't strategic about the sale."

And because of their lack of focus and imagination in marketing, most nearshore companies have started to look and sound alike. They are essentially singing from the same songbook.

And what, exactly, are they saying?

Nearshore companies across the American continent have started to "differentiate" themselves with the selling points that every other nearshore company is using.

1. Same Time Zone

The number one advantage that most, if not all, nearshore outsourcing companies tout as their most important benefit is the time zone. This plays perfectly to the pain that U.S. IT executives experience when they stay up late to make phone calls to their development teams in Bangalore or Manila. Latin American outsourcing providers emphasize the advantages of being in the same time zone as U.S. executives, who no longer have to stay late after work, or get up at an ungodly hour in the morning just to talk to their development team.

In fact, with the rise of agile software development methodologies, such as SCRUM, that require daily stand-up meetings before the workday starts, the benefits of having outsourced teams located in the same time-zone have become self-evident.

2. Similar Culture

This argument – one that plays into the fears of "the other" – is that Latin American outsourcing teams share the same western cultural values as their American customers.

But these cultural values are typically not defined. "Similar culture" loosely refers to sharing similar musical tastes, similar family values, and other fuzzy similarities. But the main benefit emphasized is that Latin American team members aren't afraid to disagree with their American clients. They're not afraid to say 'no' when, in their professional opinion, the client is clearly wrong.

They contrast this to Asia-based teams who are depicted as being "yes men," afraid to go against the wishes of their U.S. –based clients. This argument leverages cultural prejudices effectively while walking a moral fuzzy line.

3. Proximity

Trips to Asia – and even to Eastern Europe – are exhausting and take up far more time than most executives are comfortable with. You lose a whole day traveling to your destination, and another full day traveling back home. That's two days lost!

Latin American companies have skillfully played into the pain of travel across time zones. They stress the benefits of proximity when outsourcing to destinations from Mexico and Central America.

"You can get here in three hours, visit your team for a day, go to the beach the next day, and then fly back to be with your family before the weekend arrives."

A very attractive benefit, indeed, except it doesn't work for a huge swathe of outsourcing destinations. Namely everything in the southern cone, such as Brazil, Argentina, Uruguay, Chile, and Peru. Flying from New

York to Buenos Aires is about 11 hours – four hours less than a flight to London!

4. Mexico and NAFTA

Companies from Mexico have an additional advantage over other Latin American countries: their inclusion in the North American Free Trade Agreement (NAFTA). Hopefully, this won't change under the current U.S. presidential administration.

The non-immigrant NAFTA Professional (TN) visa allows citizens of Canada and Mexico, as NAFTA professionals, to work in the United States in prearranged business activities for U.S. or foreign employers. They can avoid going through the H1B visa application process.

Mexican companies can send complete teams on-site to work for up to three years, if needed. An incredible benefit for companies that have outsourced long, complex, multi-year projects and need the expertise and consistency of a team working on a continuous basis.

These are great benefits, but unfortunately, over the years they have become the same benefits used by many other outsourcing organizations throughout Latin America. They have been overused to the point where any U.S.-based company looking for nearshore outsourcing help will start to see the same benefits repeated again and again.

Most nearshore companies look just like each other, because they're all playing from the same playbook.

The "Me, Me, Me" Marketing Mistake

The most important mistake nearshore outsourcing companies make is that they talk about themselves *first*. In marketing, that is the biggest mistake one can make.

You see, customers don't care what you do. They don't care how you do it. They don't care what advantages you provide – until they're convinced you can help them solve their problem. They need to see themselves in your website, in the words of your sales people, and in your email messages or cold calls. By talking about the advantages of nearshore vs. offshore outsourcing as your main message, most nearshore companies miss the most important message they can communicate: WIIFM.

WIIFM are the English initials for: What's in it for Me.

To get somebody to notice you in the first place, you have to bridge an important gap in your prospect's mind. That gap is the gap from where your prospect is right now – a situation of pain, discomfort, dissatisfaction, unhappiness – to the place where they want to be.

How do you craft a message that communicates WIIFM? We discuss this in chapter one.

Overreliance on Government Support

Nearshore Americas, in the interview with Kops mentioned above, said, "In Latin America, as in other parts of the world, the heavy lifting when it comes to marketing outsourcing opportunities is done by government and industry organizations."

When I first became acquainted with the nearshore concept in 2009, I became aware of a program called TechBA, an initiative by the Mexican government to help Mexican technology companies enter the U.S. and Canadian markets. They had offices in Austin, Texas, San Jose, California, Detroit, Michigan, and Toronto, Canada. It was a great idea and I was happy to see the Mexican government investing money to support their growing technology industry.

However, as I became more familiar with TechBA and the companies that had been chosen to participate in the program, I started to notice a pattern – an overreliance on government support that had the effect of removing the necessity of companies investing in their own marketing.

Accelerators

TechBA was one of several accelerators dedicated to helping Latin American technology consulting companies and technology startups with their market entry into the U.S. market.

Unfortunately, TechBA no longer exists. But, there are other accelerators, such as the famous IT Clusters of Tijuana, Monterrey, Guadalajara, Cancun, and other Mexican states. There are accelerators in Argentina, Colombia, Costa Rica, Chile, and many other countries.

Accelerators were formed to create an environment for companies to learn and gain the support needed to grow their companies. But many IT management and software development firms have gotten complacent and view the accelerator and the government agency as their "marketing arm."

They have forgotten that **marketing is the prime function of a business,** as the 21st century's foremost business thinker, Peter Drucker, said in his book *The Practice of Management,* "Because it is its purpose to create a customer, any business enterprise has two-and only these two-basic functions: marketing and innovation. They are the entrepreneurial functions. Marketing is the distinguishing, the unique function of the business. A business is set apart from all other human organizations by the fact that it markets a product or a service...(a)ny organization in which marketing is either absent or incidental is not a business and should never run as if it were one."

So many nearshore technology and services companies have this false sense of comfort because they have essentially outsourced their marketing to government accelerators, even though these accelerators explicitly state that marketing should be the function of the company themselves.

Something must have been lost in translation.

Country Pavilions at International Events

Another government crutch is the company mission trip to foreign conferences or trade shows, the hallmark of which is the *country pavilion.* During the South by Southwest Interactive annual conference in Austin, Texas, several countries buy large blocks of trade show space to provide booths for companies that were carefully chosen for these trips.

At the recent 2017 SXSW, Mexico had the Promexico Pavilion, Korea had the KOCCA Pavilion, the UK had the UK Department of International Trade, and Argentina had Argentina @ SXSW – Ideas that Feed pavilion.

Country Mission Trips

Similar to the country pavilions, the country mission trip is another sponsored trip wherein a few companies have been specifically selected, out of a pool of dozens, if not hundreds, of prospective companies. The purpose of these trips is to *tour* the target country through a series of pre-arranged meetings and events designed to introduce them to new markets.

Again, this overreliance on the government to arrange these trips provides a kind of reliance, and also stigmatizes the companies involved. The message being broadcast to the target international market is, "Come and meet me because I am from Mexico/Argentina/Chile/Costa Rica…" What gets lost is the specific value proposition of each company, and how they communicate the WIIFM of target clients.

Don't get me wrong, most of the participating companies do provide a lot of value, but the message is wrong. Potential clients are not looking for vendors from a particular country, they're looking to solve a particular problem.

Overreliance on Hiring Sales People

This is a common approach that I've seen too many nearshore outsourcing providers take, and it often ends in failure. It's based on the belief that by hiring *expert* sales people to sell your services, you, the technical founder, can focus on what you do best – running a development shop/call center/BPO operation – and the "expert" will sell for you.

The problem is, you're putting the cart before the horse. There are many things that must come before you hire sales people.

First, you as the founder, must do your own initial sales. Yes, you heard right. There is no better sales person than the founder. That's true of technology startups, retail stores, consulting companies, and consumer goods.

Why should the founder do the initial sale? Because the founder knows the product or service. He or she is the only one who has the tolerance and patience to figure out the right sales pitch, the right value proposition, and is the only one who has the power and flexibility to change the offering to match the realities of the market.

Once the founder has figured out how to sell the product, then – and only then – does he have the right to ask a hired sales person to sell his product/service. It is the founder's job, either by himself or with his co-founders, to train his sales people in how to sell the service.

You're hiring sales professionals, not miracle workers.

Secondly, you need to figure out your value proposition, your positioning vis-à-vis the competition, your discounts or entry offers, and many other things before you hire sales people. This is the function of marketing (whether the founder does it or not), and must be in place before the sales person can properly sell the service.

Overreliance on Commission-Only Sales Schemes

By far, the biggest error nearshore outsourcers make – and the most unrealistic marketing/sales approach they look to – is the belief that they can hire a commission-only sales person. They do this in the mistaken belief that talented independent sales people with lots of connections will gladly introduce them to clients or even close deals for them, and the sales person won't mind receiving compensation until after the outsourcing deal has been closed.

If you believe that fairy tale, there is a bridge in Brooklyn I'd like to sell you.

Putting the shoe on the other foot, let me ask you this: would you be happy offering up your valuable Java-programmers or UX design people for a three-month assignment, free of charge, and if the application works as advertised then, and only then, would your client pay? No. You wouldn't accept that, would you? Then why would you think somebody would sell your services on a commission-only basis – especially if your service has never before been sold in the U.S. market?

Results of the Traditional Approach

So, what's the verdict on the traditional sales and marketing approach that has typified the nearshore outsourcing industry? There are five results (or lack of results) I've seen:

Unreliable or Unrepeatable Sales

The number one disadvantage I've seen with most nearshore firms, with no well-thought-out sales and marketing strategy, is the lack of a reliable or repeatable sales process. They've closed a few sales, and maybe gained an important client or two in the U.S. market, but they don't really know how they closed the sale, and are unable to repeat the steps they took to close their first one or two sales.

Feast or Famine

That lack of a repeatable sales process leads to a feast or famine mentality. Maybe you've closed a large services deal that lasts nine months and represents 75% of your total revenues, but when the project is over it's time to scramble for a new client. You're forced to put your best developers on the bench or, worse yet, lay them off.

No Presence in the Media

Today, many companies generate interest and leads through mentions in the press. There's nothing like a third party endorsement to drive interest in your company. But without a concerted sales, marketing, and PR effort, most nearshore firms have no presence in the media.

Barely Any Online Presence

Of course, today, without a solid digital presence you might as well not exist. According to the Corporate Executive Board, 57% of the purchase decision has already been completed by B2B buyers before they ever contact a sales rep. That means they've done their research online. If you don't have solid content, thought leadership, and an SEO strategy, you basically don't exist on the internet. You won't show up in your prospect's research.

At the same time, if you are already in a sales process with a U.S. company, what's the first thing they'll do? They'll Google you. If you have a bare-bones website with me-too content – or worse, if your site is in Spanish, or it's been translated badly – and you haven't published any thought leadership content that educates your prospects on their problem and your understanding of how to solve it, your chances of proving your authority to this prospect are next to none.

Not Meeting Your Potential

Finally, by not carrying out a concerted marketing and sales strategy, you are missing your potential as a company. You could be earning more revenue, closing more sales, gaining more recognition and establishing your company as a leader in your space.

It's easy to do, because nobody else is doing this. But, it takes work.

What do all the previously mentioned tactics have in common? They minimize the importance of marketing.

The Nearshore Marketing Approach

Latin American companies have access to a secret formula that will help pull the rug out from under established outsourcers and help you compete in a modern, stealthy manner. This secret formula can help you become the Netflix to outsourcing's Blockbuster; the AirBNB to outsourcing's Hilton; the Uber to outsourcing's Yellow Cab Co.

The secret to achieving breakthrough results is to realize a core truth: the rules that launched WiPro, TCS, HCL and Infosys to the top of the outsourcing game won't work for you. They got to where they are by becoming **outsourcers**.

You need to play by your own rules. You need to *stop being an outsourcing company.* As Peter Drucker said, "You're not really in the business of software development, outsourced customer support, business process outsourcing. **You're in the business of marketing."**

Now, you may be thinking, "But, we're an engineering company . . . I have an engineering degree . . . software development is what I do. How can I be a marketing company?"

That's great! I don't want you to change it. Just realize that software development, business process outsourcing, or whatever it is you do is what you deliver *after* you've performed the marketing function and created a customer.

Your service is the vehicle to help your customers achieve whatever it is they want to achieve in their lives or their businesses. Your prime function is marketing.

That's a huge mind shift, and it is what will finally make the difference for Latin American outsourcers.

To succeed as a Latin American outsourcing company, you need to stop being an outsourcing company and become a marketing company.

That's the secret formula for launching Latin America into the public imagination. Those are the new rules of the game that will help you dominate.

What is Marketing?

Before we get into the details of the Nearshore Marketing Approach, let me first define marketing for you. There are so many definitions out there about what marketing is that it gets confusing.

When you Google "What is marketing?" you get this definition: "[Marketing is] the action or business of promoting and selling products or services, including market research and advertising."

That's a very basic definition of marketing, and it's not very powerful. The American Marketing Association defines marketing as follows: "Marketing is the activity, set of institutions, and processes for creating, communicating, delivering, and exchanging offerings that have value for customers, clients, partners, and society at large."

Good definition, but a little complex.

My favorite definition by far is by Ryan Deiss of DigitalMarketer.com, "The role of marketing is to move prospects and customers through each phase of the value journey."

Why do I love this definition? Because marketing doesn't stop with awareness of who you are and what your product or service is. It doesn't stop with getting a lead. Marketing starts with that, but then it helps you take customers down your sales funnel (with your sales people), and it helps you close the sale. It helps your customers discover all the other services and products you offer, and it helps turn them into loyal customers.

Finally, marketing generates raving fans who will promote your business to other customers.

Do you see, then, why your core function should be marketing? Because marketing doesn't just stop at the awareness stage. It infuses your sales process, your product or service delivery process, your customer service process, and your retention process.

If you're a technology consulting company or a back-office outsourcing company, your technical or operational services are the tools that marketing uses to turn new customers into repeat customers, convinces your repeat customers to spend more, and then turns them into raving fans.

Nearshore Marketing Explained

But there is a special approach that you, as an outsourcing provider from Latin America can adopt when entering international markets, especially if you're trying to sell your services in the United States, Canada, and Europe. It's a secret formula I call the *Nearshore Marketing Approach.*

It's a full-spectrum marketing methodology that takes

your prospects and customers through the complete customer journey. But, it has some additional benefits to help you overcome some of the barriers particular to Latin American firms trying to enter the North American market.

Following are a few of those barriers.

Being a Foreign Company

As a company from Mexico, Argentina, Colombia, Costa Rica, Jamaica, or the Dominican Republic, you're a foreign company to U.S. prospects. That's a fact you can't hide from. It presents some barriers – but also some advantages.

Your most obvious markets are companies and organizations looking for outsourcing providers. They want to outsource their software development or back-office operations to a company in the third world to take advantage of labor-cost benefits. This is called *comparative advantage.*

Comparative advantage is an economic theory whereby one organization has an advantage over others in producing a particular good if they can produce that good at a lower relative opportunity cost, i.e., at a lower relative marginal cost prior to trade. Companies from Apple to Nike actively search out the comparative advantage when outsourcing the production of their iPhones and athletic footwear to producers in the third world.

India has developed a reputation as *the* place to outsource IT management and software outsourcing, because of their comparative advantage providing quality technology talent at a relatively low cost compared to U.S. technical talent.

Unfortunately, today, there are two disadvantages if you're a foreign company trying to do business in the outsourcing market: 1. Outsourcing has become somewhat of a dirty word, especially in today's political climate, and 2. Latin America is still a relatively unknown destination for outsourcing, despite the rise of the term "nearshore" and the marketing efforts behind this term.

While there is a small group of companies who are aware of the nearshore phenomenon and actively seek out providers from Latin America, they're just the tip of the iceberg when it comes to potential customers.

The 'Red Ocean' of Nearshore

Nearshore outsourcing has created its own red ocean, and the majority of Latin American outsourcing providers are swimming in the bloody waters of the nearshore red ocean.

In the book *Blue Ocean Strategy,* W. Chan Kim and Renée Muaborgne introduce the concept of blue oceans and red oceans. Red oceans are markets that are already full of competitors all trying to sell similar services to the same limited market. The waters within that market are red because of the bloody competition. "Products become commodities, and cutthroat competition turns the red ocean bloody."[1]

That's where the nearshore market is today. So, what's the answer?

Sell in the blue ocean – a market that's wide open. Your fellow nearshore providers are not competing against you in the blue ocean. It's a market of prospects who aren't necessarily looking for outsourcing providers, and in fact might not even be aware that outsourcing to Latin America even exists!

These are prospects and customers who have a need for your service, and you must figure out a way to connect with them and convince them that you're the answer to their prayers.

How do you, as a foreign company, connect with these North American buyers in a way that meets them where they are? How do you make that stretch and promote your services, not as a company where being from Latin America is your main asset, but as a company that has a product or service your customers want and you just *happen to be from Latin America?*

The Nearshore Marketing Approach addresses this.

Lack of understanding of the North American Market

There is a second barrier for foreign companies wanting to enter the U.S. market: your lack of understanding, or perceived lack of understanding, of the North American market and the mindset of U.S. and Canadian customers.

I've spoken to many executives from Latin American companies who express frustration at the U.S. market. They see the contradictory nature of the market: the U.S. is a huge market, but the U.S. consumer is so hard to reach and so hard to convince. The big question on every nearshore outsourcer's lips is: how do we get them to answer our phone calls or respond to our emails? How do we turn an initial meeting into subsequent meetings, and how do we close the sale?

In other words, how do we sell to a U.S. customer?

I understand the frustration. As a former enterprise sales executive, I had to learn how to break the barrier that so many companies from Latin America face. The barriers are:

1. **Lack of time.** U.S. buyers are just too busy. They ignore your email messages, your phone calls, and your trade show booths. They have no time to listen to your pitch, because they're mind-bogglingly busy just trying to deal with their own day-to-day battles.

2. **They're overwhelmed with choices.** You're just one of hundreds of vendors clamoring for their time. They get pitched electronically, via phone, and at events every day –dozens of times a day. You've got to be really damned special or relevant to be able to penetrate that barrier of indifference they've erected to keep out the ever-increasing avalanche of marketing messages.

3. **They don't want to meet you.** In Latin America, business relationships start with a meeting and end with a meeting. In the U.S., business relationships start online, and they *might* meet you at some later time in the process, if at all. If you read points one and two above, you'll see they have little time, and they're overwhelmed by vendors wanting their time.

4. **They prefer online.** Closely related to the previous point, American buyers start their buying process online. In fact, the corporate executive board noted that 57% of the purchase decision has been completed by B2B buyers before they ever contact a sales rep.

The Nearshore Marketing approach addresses these barriers, especially points two and four above: how to penetrate the wall of indifference U.S. buyers erect to protect themselves from the constant stream – or spam – of vendors trying to sell to them, and how to form a compelling, authoritative online presence that will help you get to the 57% stage with your prospects.

The Components of the Nearshore Marketing Process

So, I know I've kept you waiting a long time, and you're probably saying to yourself, "All right, tell me, already! What is this secret nearshore marketing formula?"

Okay, I hear you . . . thanks for your patience!

I'll summarize here the components of the nearshore marketing process, and I'll delve into the details in each subsequent chapter.

1. How to Position Your Service in the U.S. Market

In chapter one we'll explain that you should position yourself by emphasizing the *transformation* you provide your customers, not by emphasizing the service you sell. Yes, you heard me right. Nobody cares about your product or service. Yet, we, as entrepreneurs, fall in love with what we sell, and we talk about what we sell all the time.

Your customers are not buying your product or service – they're buying a transformation. They live in a place of dissatisfaction and pain. They want to get to a new destination, a place where life is better, where they're smarter, better looking, more powerful, and more successful. Sell them that transformation and know that your product or service is just the vehicle to get them there.

In this chapter we explain how to position your offerings as the vehicle to help your customers achieve the transformation they're looking for.

2. Your Number One Marketing Tool

In chapter two we discuss why your customer's journey with your company and your service is your number one marketing tool. Marketing doesn't end with convincing prospects to become customers. As such, you must infuse marketing into how you deliver your services.

How you on-board your customers, how you deliver your service or product, how you support your customers when they have questions or problems, how you upsell them and cross-sell them, and eventually, how you turn them into members of your "tribe" is all marketing. In this chapter, I'll teach you how to turn your company's operations and processes into powerful marketing vehicles.

3. How to Establish Authority to Make Selling Easy

In chapter three I'll explain the importance of establishing authority with content and how to develop that authority. Authority is especially important when you're a foreign company entering the U.S. market and you're a completely unknown entity. Establishing authority helps to break the barrier of being an unknown organization and establishes you as a thought leader in your space.

4. The Right Way to Build Your Website

In chapter four we explain why most nearshore companies entering the U.S. market use their website in the wrong way. They think their website exists to explain what they do and list their services. What I argue in this chapter is that your website is a resource that should combine the functionality of an app, an educational resource (to fulfill your customer's information gathering needs), and as a tool to get them to the next stage using calls-to-action and sales funnels.

5. How to Drive Traffic to Your Website

In chapter five we explain how to drive traffic to your website through paid and organic methods. In this day and age, even if you sell a high-end B2B product or service that requires a high-touch, person-to-person sales process, ignoring traffic to your web properties is like missing one leg of a three-legged stool. You need a steady stream of prospects, thought leaders, influencers, and industry pundits coming to your website through various means.

I'll explain how to leverage your content to produce earned media attention, how to drive traffic using modern SEO methods, and how to leverage paid advertising to get the flow of traffic started to your authority content assets.

6. Selling 2.0: How to Reach The Right Customers

In chapter six I explain the importance of reaching out directly to your prospects through direct mail and other outbound methods. These are called contact campaigns, a term coined by author and consultant Stu Heinecke.

As B2B companies selling high-end services, it doesn't do you any good to wait for your prospects to contact you. You have a much smaller addressable market than B2C companies. You can probably identify all your prospects on one spreadsheet. While it's essential to drive traffic to your content, it's mandatory to reach out directly to your customers, especially if you know who they are. In this chapter, we explain how to design and execute a contact campaign to generate leads and customers.

7. How to Close More Sales With the Escalation Model

In the final chapter, chapter seven, I explain the importance of selling your service through the escalation model instead of the traditional way. What is the escalation method? Just as you can't ask someone to marry you right after you meet them at a party (you have to actually date that person, and progress through various stages of the dating process before you get to pop the question), you also can't immediately start pitching your service.

In this chapter, I explain the psychology behind the escalation method, and how to build a predictable sales model by taking your prospects through logical, sequential steps so your customers see that buying your core service is a logical next step.

How to Use This Book

To get the most out of this book, I recommend reading it all the way through, from beginning to end. Get a feel for the methodology, and start thinking about how this could apply to your own business.

After your first pass, then it's time to implement the steps I outline in each chapter. I would start with Chapter 7, "Sell Your Service with the Escalation Method," and Chapter 1, "Sell a Transformation, Not Your Service." You need to define *what you're actually selling, and how to sell it,* before you perform any other type of marketing.

These first two chapters form the basis of your entrepreneurial journey in the U.S. market. Michael Masterson, in his book *Ready, Fire, Aim,* says, "Without sales, it is very hard to sustain an ongoing business."

Then I would go straight to Chapter 6, "Outbound Marketing is Alive and Well." You need your first few clients, and the best way to get them is to reach out directly, don't wait for them to come to you.

Then you should immediately go to Chapter 3, "Establish Authority Through Your Content." To sustain an ongoing sales rhythm, you need to establish authority through content. Having authority content will make your sales process easier and smoother. It's like oil to lubricate your sales machine.

Then proceed to build out a useful, functional, "app-like" website through the recommendations in Chapter 4, drive traffic to it using the recommendations from Chapter 5, and finally, once you have enough customers and you start delivering your services, laser focus on applying the recommendations in Chapter 2.

[1] Kim, W. Chan; Kim, W. Chan; Mauborgne, Renee; Mauborgne, Renée A. (2014-01-20). Blue Ocean Strategy, Expanded Edition: How to Create Uncontested Market Space and Make the Competition Irrelevant (p. 4). Harvard Business Review Press.

1

HOW TO
POSITION YOUR
SERVICE IN THE
U.S. MARKET

"Nobody cares about your products (Except You)" —
David Meerman Scott

Don't sell your product or service.

Yes, you heard me right. Nobody cares about what you sell. They don't care about your proprietary methodology. They don't care about your agile development practices and how many scrum masters you have. They don't care if you're a CMMI Level 5. They couldn't care less what languages, platforms, and technologies your people are experts in.

Does what I'm saying sound sacrilegious or stupid? I know you've spent a lot of time hiring the best developers, expert java programmers, UX/UI gurus. Your customers demand it. Right?

Don't get me wrong. Yes, this stuff is important – but not right now. Not when you're trying to attract prospects.

The problem with most outsourcing providers today is that they make their expertise, their certifications and their qualifications the first thing they sell to customers. They believe that's what people are really buying.

But all that is a commodity. Expertise, certifications, technology, methodologies: they're all commodities. They're a dime a dozen. Everybody in your space sells this. So, what?

As I mentioned in the introduction, American executives – and most executives in the world – are overwhelmed by people selling to them. Their inboxes are full of sales pitches. Their executive assistants are shielding them from dozens of cold calls a day from people trying to sell the same stuff as you.

When vendors talk non-stop about methodologies, technologies, processes, certifications, years of experience, and awards, it just turns into a wall of noise.

Here's a statement I copied from the website of a Latin American software development outsourcing company:

"We offer world-class services through agile or traditional

methodologies by relying on the most talented pool of engineers in the region."

Let me provide the translated text; the one the U.S.-based executive sees:

"We offer blah blah blah blah blah blah blah . . . "

There's a good chance your message is getting lost in translation. The message you're pitching to U.S. prospects probably sounds a lot like the "blah blah blah" translation I provided above. Although I was being facetious, that really is how the majority of messages come across.

When you start with explaining your products and services, your prospect's eyes start to glaze over. They're clicking the browser back button, deleting the email, hanging up on your phone call, and walking away from the trade-show booth that your country's ministry of external commerce spent so much money to sponsor.

Ouch!

I know this might rub a lot of people the wrong way, but it needs to be said. Let me repeat it: **Nobody cares about your methodology, your certifications, your 'same time-zone, same culture' proximity.**

Not yet anyway.

Your Customers Want Transformation

The key to getting through the impenetrable Great Wall of China your prospects have erected, the way to unscramble the voice scrambler that turns your beautiful product and service pitch into just garbled noise, is to sell a transformation.

To illustrate my point, let's turn to the most successful Super Bowl ad ever: The 1984 Apple Macintosh commercial.

Apple 1984 Super Bowl Ad

You can watch the ad here: https://youtu.be/VtvjbmoDx-I

In this ad, in which Apple introduces the first ever Macintosh computer, we see a dystopian future with a dictator speaking from a screen to a zombie-like mass of people. Suddenly a lone, athletic woman, the only person in color in a black and white scene, runs down the passageway and throws a mallet at the screen, disrupting the rally and shattering the hypnotic hold the dictator has on the crowd.

The message is one of transformation. Apple, represented

by the athletic woman, is freeing the masses from the corporate conformity that existed at the time (a subtle jab at IBM). The woman (Apple) represents freedom of expression, the freedom to be creative, the freedom to be yourself.

Conspicuously absent from the commercial was any mention of CPU speed, memory, and hard drive capacity, software features, or anything technical. And that was the brilliance of the commercial: it purposefully avoided any talk of technology, choosing to focus instead on transformation.

This sounds well and good for consumer goods, but how can serious B2B companies sell transformation?

We must first realize that B2B is still P2P – people-to-people. People make decisions to buy your products, and each person is his or her own universe. Each director of development, chief technology officer, chief operations officer, director of engineering, or IT manager is a human being with desires, dreams, issues, and challenges.

Maslow's Hierarchy of Needs

To identify how to sell transformation, you need to realize that most decisions are made emotionally, and then justified through logic. Even when it comes to enterprise consulting or BPM services, there is always a core emotional element. These emotional elements are the most powerful levers you can pull to influence who buys your products or services.

A tool to help you identify the transformation you need to sell is Maslow's Hierarchy of Needs.

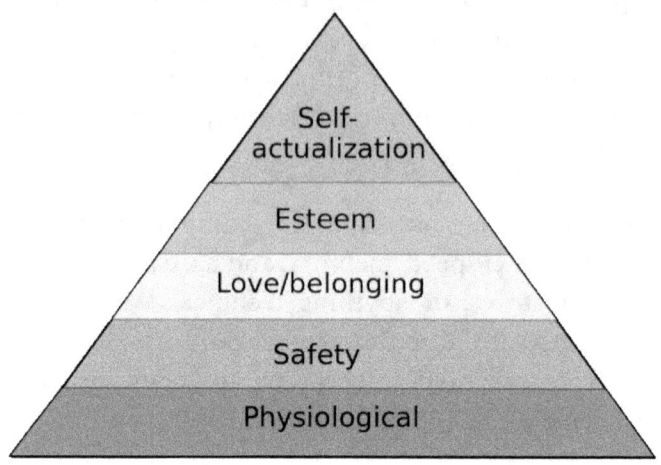

In his 1943 paper, "A Theory of Human Motivation," published in *Psychological Review,* Abraham Maslow described a pyramid of needs that progresses from the most basic needs to the most sophisticated. First are physiological and safety needs, which include food, water, shelter, safety from danger, and so on. These are the needs the earliest human cave dwellers struggled to satisfy.

We still seek to satisfy them today, except today we're not battling sabre tooth tigers – we're battling crime, financial security, disease, and our own demons.

Then we get into social belonging, such as friendships, intimacy, and family. Maslow realized humans need to belong to social groups, whether through clubs, families, organizations, sports teams, or gangs. We also need to experience love, such as familial love and sexual love.

After we've satisfied our belonging and friendship needs, our next level of needs are self-esteem and self-confidence. This includes status, the respect of others, recognition, fame, prestige, competence, mastery, independence, and freedom.

Next is self-actualization. This level of need refers to a person's full potential and the realization of that potential. Maslow describes this level as the desire to accomplish everything that one can, to become the most that one can be. The U.S. Army used this very effectively during the 1990s to recruit people during a time of relative peace and security in the world. "Be All You Can Be" became the U.S. Army's most recognized slogan, even to this day.

The Gap

All of us humans are in a struggle to reach a destination that was previously unreachable, whether in our personal lives or in our careers. Maslow's Hierarchy of Needs is the best tool I've seen to describe where we are in that struggle to achieve something, to transform ourselves, to go from here to there.

To sell transformation then, you need to identify the gap between your customer's "before" and "after" state, and identify their core needs and emotions related to the gap between their "before" and "after" state.

Your service, whether it's software development, captive data centers, outsourced accounting, customer support, or whatever it is you deliver, is **just a vehicle to bridge**

the gap for your customers between their "before" state to their "after" state.

How do you identify your customer's gap?

Where They Are Now

Identify where your customers are now. What do they lack in their world, in their work, in their personal and professional lives? What do their companies lack? What is bothering them? What constraints are keeping them from reaching their goals?

For example, your customers might be financial services providers, like insurance companies, who don't yet have a way for their customers to interact with their insurance policies and pay their bills via an online app. The company receives complaint after complaint that their website is difficult to use on their mobile phones, and that it's inconvenient to pay their bills and print out new insurance identification cards because they can only use a computer or laptop, not their mobile phones.

The director of customer service's inbox is inundated with angry emails from customers complaining about how user-unfriendly their website is, and how they wish the company provided them with an easy-to-use app to manage their accounts from their phones.

Emotions

The above scenario causes a lot of emotions for our embattled customer service director. How do you think she's feeling? She might be experiencing a combination of emotions, such as feeling overwhelmed, frustrated, tired, scared. She's scared that her boss might fire her for all the complaints. She's frustrated at the workload her people have and by how many issues get escalated to her. She's overwhelmed at the amount of work awaiting her every day when she comes into the office.

A Day in the Life

Next, what is the day-in-the-life of our customer service director? She's harried, running to put out one fire after another. She doesn't have enough time to work on the strategic stuff she needs to do to design a perfect customer service journey since her staff is handling complaints all day long.

She's probably working long hours, staying late four out of five days of the week, and maybe working some weekends.

Status

Here's where we're getting into heavy Maslow territory. Is our customer service director getting a lot of respect right now? Probably not from her staff and customers. Is she self-actualized? Probably not. She never imagined she would be putting out fires instead of working at her dream job designing ideal customer experiences and becoming the company's hero.

The Enemy

Yes, there is an enemy and each person battles that enemy every day.

For our customer service director at the insurance

company, her enemy is the support queue. The support queue should be non-existent if she had the right technology in place – a modern mobile app that works on iPhones as well as Android phones. An app that's fully integrated with their back-end ERP systems. Instead, because her customers are interacting with her company's website through their phone's browsers – and the experience is not optimized for mobile – her day is filled with the evil empire called "The Support Queue."

Once you're able to identify where your customers are now, as well as all the emotions, daily activities, status, and the enemies they battle, you can very clearly see how you can help your customers experience transformation.

Where They Want to Go

Each of the previous points has an opposite. From where they are now, to where they want to go. Marketer Russell Brunson says to be cautious, however.

People don't want improvement, they want *a complete change*.

When I mentioned transformation at the beginning of this chapter, I wasn't referring to incremental improvement. I was referring to a new place, a new destination, a renewal, a reinvention.

Improvement is hard. It takes effort and it doesn't yield much. Transformation is a complete change. It's the fantasy that you can leave it all behind and enter a new world.

People   buy   transformation.   They   don't   buy

improvement. They secretly desire throwing away their old lives and adopting new ones. That's exciting. The problem is that getting better where they are right now is slow, tedious, and just more of the same.

They want to be like a caterpillar that enters a chrysalis and emerges two weeks later as a beautiful monarch butterfly.

Offer them the chrysalis.

What types of transformation are companies looking for today?

- They want to become internet companies
- They want to become software-powered companies
- They want to be the dominant companies in their industry
- They want to grow 10X faster than they have been
- They want to sell their companies for billions of dollars
- They want to become the "Uber" of their industry
- They want to become the "Amazon" of their industry

We're always being told that companies buy things for four reasons: 1. They want to increase revenues; 2. They want to decrease costs; 3. They want to increase market share; 4. They want to decrease risk.

Those are the four logical reasons companies will use to justify their purchases, but, what really sells is emotion, and to get somebody emotionally sold on your product you need to sell the transformation.

So, where do they want to go? Let's look at the insurance company example I mentioned earlier. They don't have a way for customers to use an app to pay their bills, consult their policies, and make changes.

What are they looking to do? Well . . . yes, they want an app. That's what you might be able to build for them. But what do they really want?

They want to become an internet company.

A software powered company.

The dominant company in their industry.

What does the decision-maker you're trying sell to really want? If she's the customer service director, she might want to achieve something so breakthrough that she would be considered as the next VP of Operations or maybe the next COO.

Or she might be positioning herself to be hired by a competitor or a company in a different industry as one of their top executives. Think Marissa Mayer, who was a rising star at Google, and then became CEO of Yahoo in 2012.

Emotions

What emotions would your target prospect experience after achieving the transformation? How about feeling exhilarated, triumphant, free, powerful? Really identify the emotions your prospect will feel when achieving the transformation they are seeking. It's the key to making the sale.

A Day in the Life

What would the day in the life of our hero be? Busy, but relaxed? Her day completely organized by an executive assistant, with time for a few meetings, time for creative work, and time for busy work, but not chaotic like before? Maybe her days would be spent evangelizing her company's message through speaking engagements, interviews, blogging, and meeting with VIPs every day?

Status

How would her status change after getting the transformation she's looking for? Would she become the hero of her company? The poster-child for innovative thinking? The model employee, manager, or director?

The Enemy

The enemy has been defeated. The support queue has been tamed by a powerful, innovative methodology provided by her outsourcing provider (that's you!). It runs like a well-oiled machine, and there are no emergencies. The support queue yields valuable information about issues that can help her help the company with product planning, process optimization, and new market opportunities.

The enemy has been transformed into an ally, and is no longer an enemy.

2

YOUR NUMBER ONE MARKETING TOOL

"Creating a new customer is fundamental. It's sexy. And keeping a customer is also fundamental. It's not sexy." – Jeffrey Eisenberg

You've heard the old refrain: it's more expensive to acquire a new customer than to sell to a current customer. Well, it's true. In fact, to maximize profitability, smart companies try to establish a business based on repeat business through a core tribe of fanatical, dedicated clients.

Today, the bar has been set very high. Companies like

Zappos (acquired by Amazon), Ritz-Carlton, and Nordstrom have been setting new standards in customer satisfaction.

But the company really blazing the trail is Amazon. Not Apple. Not Uber. Not Google. It's Amazon. They've perfected the art of turning their core service into their number one marketing tool.

In their recent book, *Be Like Amazon: Even a Lemonade Stand Can Do It,* Bryan & Jeffrey Eisenberg, together with Roy Williams discussed the four pillars of Amazon and the powerful force for growth they've created in the way they deliver their service.

In the book, they describe what they refer to as Amazon's 'Unifying Principles' (their term, not Jeff Bezos' term). These unifying principles are:

1. Customer Centricity
2. Continuous Optimization
3. Culture of Innovation
4. Corporate Agility

For the rest of this chapter I'll go over each of these items and their importance in delivering a service that becomes a powerful marketing tool for your company.

Customer Centricity

Jay Baer, in his book *Hug Your Haters,* cited a Forrester study that found that 80% of businesses believed they deliver "superior" customer service. The same study found that only 8% of customers agree their service is superior. That's a huge disconnect. As business owners, we believe we deliver great service, and our customers have a wonderful experience during their interactions with our company.

Amazon has turned that into one of their core principles. They live and breathe by customer-centricity.

The Eisenberg Brothers and Williams cite a famous example from Amazon's early days, when it was a bookseller exclusively (and not selling everything under the sun, like they do today). In the mid to late '90s Amazon's employees wrote almost all of the book reviews. Bezos instructed them to be honest about their opinions. As a result, some of the reviews were negative.

Bezos received an angry letter from a book publisher who said that Bezos didn't understand that he was in the business to sell books, not trash them. Bezos said, "When I read that letter, I thought, 'we don't make money when we sell things. We make money when we help customers make purchasing decisions.'"

From the very beginning Amazon was customer-centric. This was just one early example of how Amazon put the interests and concerns of their customers first.

But does being customer-centric work? Eisenberg, Eisenberg, and Williams analyzed the performance of the S&P 500, from 2007 to 2013, and compared the companies on the index with the companies in the Forrester Customer Experience Index, which provides a list of "Customer Service Leaders" and a list of "Customer Service Laggards." What they found should give any company pause. While the S&P 500 Index was up 14.5% in that seven-year period, the Customer Service Laggards were down 33.9%. The Customer Service Leaders, on the other hand, were up an astonishing 76.9%.

But what about profits and customer retention? How does being customer-centric help your company's bottom line? Jay Baer said in *Hug Your Haters,* "Advertising is a tax paid when you're poor at retaining your current customers."

Baer goes on to say that a 5% increase in customer retention can boost profits by 25-85%.

Culture of Innovation

Amazon's second pillar is Innovation. But not innovation for innovation's sake. It's innovation in the pursuit of customer centricity.

Take, for example, Amazon's packaging. The way you package a product for shipment would seem like a boring, innocuous feature. Just package each product so that it doesn't sustain any damage during shipping, and you're good to go.

But Amazon applied the principle of innovation in their packaging to solve a huge customer pain point: packages that were notoriously difficult to open. Just think about the number of times you've bought a physical product in a store, such as batteries or a piece of electronic equipment. The packaging is so complicated and hard to open that it causes enormous frustration.

It became the subject of a hilarious scene in the famous American sitcom *Curb Your Enthusiasm,* with Larry David trying to open a package that wouldn't open.

Larry David in epic battle with frustrating packaging

https://youtu.be/6ZIfkDG7HNM

Amazon solved an issue that had become a customer frustration by innovating their packaging. They created "Frustration Free Packaging."

Amazon's Frustration-Free Packaging

https://youtu.be/bgw3EmszzLY

The way Amazon explains Frustration Free Packaging is they created their innovation as a way to alleviate "wrap

rage." They say their packaging was designed to feature "
... products in recyclable boxes that are easy to open and
contain fewer excess materials."

How can you innovate your products – or the way you
deliver your services – so you can continue to delight
your customers and drive high customer satisfaction?

Since many nearshore outsourcing providers are in the
technology space, innovation is a central part of what
a lot of providers deliver as a service. 'Software' and
'innovation' are terms that seem to go hand in hand.

But, can you innovate a part of your service delivery
process? Can you put on your 'innovation' hat when
designing your customer on-boarding process? Your
weekly or daily communications? The way you sell your
service?

I've spoken to a few software outsourcing companies
from Latin America who have developed innovations in
the way they perform their daily stand-up meetings when
carrying out their agile or Scrum-centered software
development approach.

Daily stand-up meetings are a standard practice in
Scrum, and are often a regimented process whereby team
members, who are typically all sitting in a conference
room, must stand up when it's their turn to speak and
quickly state what they did the day (or week before), what
they'll work on today, what roadblocks are standing in
their way, and where they need help.

Often, they'll use little props when it's their turn, such as
a basketball or a hacky-sack. When it's somebody else's

turn, they'll pass the prop to the next person whose turn it is to stand up and say their piece.

For remote teams, this is not feasible. One company I worked with made up for that by using two video cameras to "simulate" the in-person stand-up meeting. They used one camera so the U.S.-based team could see their Latin American team when it was their turn to stand, and another camera pointed towards the white board showing the Kanban swim lanes.

On each side, both the U.S. location as well as the Latin American location, there was a wide-screen TV or screen where the image of the meeting was projected. The result of this innovation was a positive customer experience. The U.S.-based client felt they were working with a team that was intimately integrated with them, using the miracle of video-conferencing, not a remote team.

Continuous Optimization

Continuous optimization is closely related to innovation in Amazon's four pillars, as it is a principle used to improve their operations and products to provide excellent customer service.

Amazon is constantly searching for ways to optimize their operations, products, and services. One of the unique ways it does this is to divide their whole company into small, self-directed teams.

I wanted to include a quote direct from the book, *Be Like Amazon*, "[Jeff] Bezos has figured out how to combine the entrepreneurial culture of a small company with the financial resources of a large one. And that allows

Amazon to tackle and solve problems that other big companies can't quite wrap their arms around."

When you empower your employees to continuously improve your processes, you must be prepared to let go. You can't try to control everything they do, or else you'll stifle any innovation and optimization they can create in the service of your customers.

This has been a key organizational feature for Amazon, and it should be for you, too.

Amazon's teams are fairly small. Bezos has established a "two-pizza rule." He will not allow a team to be larger than can be fed by two pizzas.

Corporate Agility

Finally, you need to incorporate agility into your corporate culture, the fourth pillar in Amazon's unifying principles.

Agility has traditionally been associated with software development, as well as with startups.

In his book, *The Lean Startup*, Eric Ries describes a model for creating startups that is based on agility. Startups should be agile enough to change their business model, product, and approach as soon as they discover their original approach won't work. They need to be able to fail fast so they can quickly learn what will work and what won't work, before they run out of operating capital.

Today, corporations as well as small companies need to

act like startups. One of the keys to Amazon's success is their ability to turn on a dime and get rid of things that aren't working, or adopt things that are working.

There are still too many companies that are stuck in their old ways of operating. Look at Kodak, Blockbuster Video, and Borders Books. Jeffrey Eisenberg, in his blog post, *Scaling Growth,* uses the term *Risk Aversion* to describe the opposite of corporate agility (see: http://www.buyerlegends.com/scaling-growth-gift-entrepreneur/).

As a foreign company trying to make it in the world's largest market, there's no other way to operate other than as an agile company. If you find a marketing tactic, a development methodology, or a customer communications method that works better than the one you've used before, give your people the total freedom and authority to change the way you've done things in favor of the new, better way.

In fact, empower your employees to think like owners. Their response to a possible innovation that could change your company's fortunes for the better should never be, "I need to check with my boss about that." It should be, "I'll make this change now knowing my boss will approve because it's for the benefit of the customer and, consequently, for the company."

Customer Touch Points

In addition to Amazon's Four Pillars, I would like to recommend a fifth pillar promoted by nearshore customer service outsourcing firm Infolink. It's the concept of Customer Journey Support, and identifying key **customer touch points.**

José Gonzalez, Infolink CEO, has perfected the process of delivering support across the complete journey that a customer will take with your product and company. At each step of the way there are key touch points that define the relationship between your customer and your company.

These touch points include customer on-boarding, first product use, product training, continued use 30 days, 60 days, and 90 days after purchase, technical support, contract renewal, upsell and cross-well.

At each touch point you need to design an experience that will increase your customer's satisfaction, delight them, and enhance the value they derive from your company.

When you design your customer touch points to maximize their experience with your company, and you pair that with fanatical customer-centricity, continuous optimization, a culture of innovation and corporate agility, your product and/or service becomes one of the most powerful marketing tools that exists today.

3

HOW TO ESTABLISH AUTHORITY TO MAKE SELLING EASY

"It literally doesn't matter what business you're in, what industry you operate in, if you're not producing content, you basically don't exist." – Gary Vaynerchuk

As providers of outsourcing services, you're selling a big-ticket item. Whether software development, IT management, call center, or back-office services, you're closing five, six, or even seven figure contracts. Big-ticket sales require a direct, outbound sales approach. These are not sales you close with an online shopping cart and a "buy" button.

Today, this is not enough. It's not enough to just have a sales team making outbound calls, sending outbound emails, and working the conference or trade show floor. To succeed in today's world, you have to establish authority through content.

Everybody has become, or has the potential to become, a publisher. The good news is that you no longer must own a newspaper, a television station, or a radio station. The internet has given everybody the potential to have their own platform. As a result, millions of people have taken advantage of the opportunity to produce valuable content that attracts an audience and establishes them as an authority.

The internet has enabled small players, with little to no resources, to compete with and beat large, established players with millions of dollars in the bank. This opportunity is available to you – right now!

But establishing authority through content is not just an opportunity – it's a necessity. It's the price of doing business.

Marketing guru Gary Vaynerchuk's quote, listed above, is worth repeating, "It literally doesn't matter what business you're in, what industry you operate in, if you're not producing content, you basically don't exist."

Now, before you get scared that you're going to have to become a content-producing machine, publishing blog posts every week or even every day, don't worry – I won't ask you to do that (unless you want to take your content production and to the next level with a media company approach).

Creating "authority content" doesn't require publishing weekly or daily – it just requires creating valuable content that establishes you as an expert in your field.

As Brian Clark, Founder and CEO of Copyblogger said, "It really boils down to the demonstration of expertise through delivery of valuable content . . ."

Why Authority Content?

Why do you need authority content? What, apart from the fact that "everybody creates content," is the benefit of authority content?

Accelerates the Sales Process

Authority content provides the proper context for your sales efforts. If you're seen as an authority, you're more likely to have your emails answered and your calls returned.

Authority content is also a great way to start a sales call. Consider the difference between a competitor who cold-calls or cold-emails a prospect requesting a meeting, and then you email or call the same prospect, but this time you offer a book you've written (or better yet, you send a printed book to the prospect, and then follow-up with a phone call).

Who is more likely to get an appointment with the

prospect, especially if they're an important prospect from a large company? You, of course!

Helps With PR

Another reason why you should produce authority content is because it's a great way to generate PR. You get an opportunity to be mentioned in the press. Imagine you've published a report with findings from original research that your company has conducted. This report will help you get responses from journalists and writers for magazines, newspapers, or high authority blogs looking for original content to publish.

That was the case with Infochimps when they were performing a business model pivot. I explain this case in detail below.

Helps to Generate Leads

Along with your outbound sales process you must also have an inbound sales process. Key to that is generating leads by getting prospects to subscribe to your email list. The best way to get prospects to raise their hands and subscribe to your email list is to provide some sort of incentive. Marketing guru Jeff Walker calls this an *ethical bribe* in exchange for their email address. A piece of authority content, whether it's a downloadable PDF, access to a private video, or a "free + shipping" book, provides a perfect opportunity to generate leads.

Something to Share on Social Media

Companies are always looking for ways to get more followers, more shares, and more engagement on

LinkedIn, Facebook, Twitter, or any other social media. Your authority content, especially if it contains information that teaches something that people really want to learn (a complete guide to topic "x," or a free course or tutorial), then people will want to share that more than some promotional piece of content.

Offers for Paid Advertising

One of the best ways to advertise, especially if you're using some sort of pay-per-click advertising like Google AdWords, Facebook ads, or LinkedIn ads, is to advertise a piece of authority content, and not advertise your company or services right away. This is especially true if your service is very expensive and projects last anywhere between six months to two years.

Your advertising will be more effective if you advertise a book you've published, or a free report, some sort of webinar, or "free training."

Types of Authority Content

There are certain types of content that lend themselves more to providing the authority you need to attract customers than others.

Books

For providers of professional services, which is what most outsourcing companies from Latin America and the Caribbean offer U.S. companies, one of the best pieces of authority content is books. In fact, Lee Frederiksen, CEO and Founder of Hinge Marketing, a firm that specializes in marketing for professional services firms, believes that every consulting company founder or CEO should write a book.

In one of his blog posts he wrote, "'Our management team has read your book, and it really reflects what we would like to do... so obviously you are already at the top of our short list.' This is pretty much verbatim the opening line of a phone call that I received from a well-qualified prospective client last week."

Frederiksen went on to explain the prospect wasn't even on their database of target accounts. He hadn't even heard of the firm.

Books are great because of the packaging, especially if you have a paperback or hardback version of your book. You can have the same content spread out over twenty-five blog posts, but if it's published in a book, it has more prestige; more "caché."

The book *Software Without Borders* was the key that helped Steve Mezak turn his company, Accelerance, the firm he created to help U.S. executives outsource their software development, into the success it is today.

In the book, Mezak provides CIOs and directors of engineering a roadmap to outsourcing software development – while positioning himself as a leader in the space, and helping to shape the criteria for how outsourcing providers are chosen. In other words, the book educated U.S. software development executives in how to become an Accelerance client, positioning Accelerance as the *only* solution to a company's outsourcing needs.

Marketing automation provider Hubspot benefitted from publishing the book *Inbound,* co-authored by co-founders Brian Halligan and Dharmesh Shah. The book helped Hubspot coin the term "inbound marketing," and turn it into one of the most popular internet marketing methodologies today.

Now the term, inbound marketing, has become the de facto B2B marketing approach, and is intimately tied to Hubspot software through their authoritative book, as well as their popular blog.

Another marketing software provider, ClickFunnels, co-founded by marketing guru Russell Brunson, has benefitted by publishing two best-selling books: *Dotcom Secrets* and *Expert Secrets,* both authored by Russell Brunson.

Brunson uses both books as the front-end to attract every prospect through their sales funnels.

Free Reports

Reports, also referred to as white papers or eBooks, are the next type of authority content. But this is not the typical type of free report. The type of report that constitutes authority content is original research introducing new data into the marketplace of ideas.

New research is especially important when trying to establish authority with C-level executives in markets that are very data-oriented.

In 2013, Big Data provider Infochimps used this tactic to successfully pivot their business model and attract a completely different type of prospect. Originally created as a seller of data, they quickly realized companies would not spend money to obtain data, since so much of it was available for free. They were stuck with high capacity servers designed to crunch petabytes of data. They realized there was a better market opportunity offering their excess capacity as "Big Data-on demand" providers.

Their target market changed, so they had to acquire a completely new set of prospects. Their VC firm and board of directors had given them an aggressive timeline to attract hundreds of new leads and clients in their target market, leaving Marketing Director, Amanda McGuckin Hager with the task of achieving a very aggressive goal.

Partnering with the SQL Server Worldwide User Group (SSWUG), McGuckin Hager and her team surveyed SSWUG members, almost all of them database administrators, to gain intelligence about the state of big data and to identify the market opportunity.

McGuckin Hager said they commissioned the study to confirm their assumptions about big data and the cloud, but were surprised to find that most database administrators were not interested in the cloud.

What they did discover was very revealing: "Nearly 55 percent of big data projects fail."

They published the study in a report entitled *CIOs & Big Data: What Your IT Team Wants You to Know.* It was the first report of its kind providing never-before-seen stats and insight into the big data phenomenon. They also produced an infographic to support their findings.

To give the report a push, McGuckin Hager hired a PR consultant, Jeff Salzgeber, to promote it. Describing him as an "old-school" PR pro who worked the phones, Salzgeber convinced some of the most prestigious publications to write stories about the research.

The result?

The report's findings became some of the most cited research in the big data industry. In fact, the sentence, ". . . 55 percent of big data projects fail" has been quoted repeatedly by high profile publications such as *Forbes*, *Computer Weekly*, and the *Wall Street Journal*. It produces 641,000 results in Google searches.

They were also able to increase their in-house database by 94%, and their opportunity pipeline by 358%.

What lessons can we extrapolate from the Infochimps experience?

There are a few that are easy to duplicate, and some that require good timing:

Produce original research. Producing original research is a great way to establish yourself as an authority in your industry. You'll add value to your audience while distinguishing yourself from the millions of "me, too" content creators.

Work with industry associations. With about 100,000 members, SSWUG was an important factor in the report's success. Working with an industry association carries the prestige of a third-party endorsement and can give you immediate access to the members who might be a ready market for your products or services.

Don't neglect traditional PR. In our digital-first world we tend to forget that some traditional tactics still work – spectacularly well. This is especially true as we enter the age of content shock. The "build it and they will come" approach to content marketing is long dead and has been replaced by the need to actively promote your content.

Be at the right place at the right time. McGuckin Hager admitted that her timing couldn't have been better. Working for a big data provider at the cusp of the big data revolution, and publishing original research with never before seen data points, was either the result of incredible foresight or super good fortune. McGuckin Hager said she lucked into it. But as Seneca said, luck is what happens when preparation meets opportunity. McGuckin Hager is pretty damned good at what she does.

The research report mentioned here is not the end of the story. According to a case study on the website Marketing Sherpa about the Infochimps pivot (which became one of their Top 3 Inbound Marketing Case Studies of 2014), in addition to the report in question, they published content on their blog, produced six technical white papers, one how-to guide, three data sheets, six case studies, nine webinars, and seven event videos.

Finally, in 2013, they were acquired by Computer Sciences Corporation.

Power Blog Posts

Blogging has become one of those "must-haves" for any B2B company. Most nearshore companies who have committed to entering the U.S. market have some sort of blogging program. But most blog posts range between 700 and 900 words and follow a very similar format: Educate readers on a topic related to what they do, usually in a list format.

However, with a power blog post, you're writing a 2,000 to 5,000 word article providing a thorough, detailed, and authoritative approach to a topic you want to be known for.

For example, let's look at the typical list-post. A list-post can be lessons or a tutorial, and each list item is a step in a step-by-step approach. It can also be a comprehensive listing of items to inform readers of "The Best of" or "The Top____".

In a power blog post, however, you would write an *enhanced list* post. In an enhanced list post, you turn a traditional list-post into a piece of authority content. How do you structure an enhanced list post? Each item in your list is like its own mini-blog post. You not only introduce your point, but you explain in detail how to carry it out, with step-by-step instructions, diagrams, and other details.

You could also write the *Complete Guide* to your topic, or even a mini-chapter book where, instead of list items, you have chapters.

Are you starting to notice a trend? A power blog post is

almost like a white paper or eBook, but published as an extra-long blog post designed to establish you and your company as an authority in your field.

Free Trainings

Free Trainings are another, sexier, word for webinars. I use this term as it contains more value for prospective customers. Your prospects would prefer to attend a free training than a webinar. Webinars usually mean they're going to get "sold" something. Training means they're going to learn something.

More importantly, the term, "free training," sets you apart as an expert in your field.

Free trainings are an increasingly popular way to offer authority content, and are a great way to direct paid traffic from Facebook or LinkedIn ads. Use your free training to address the client pain gap we discussed in Chapter 1.

Organize the training into three parts:

> 1. First, address your understanding of the client's pain, where they are, and where they want to go. Really hammer this point home.
> 2. Then, provide in-depth training on two or three steps that can help them resolve their pain. Really pack in the value. While you're teaching, make sure to use case studies of real clients who have achieved results using the methods you're teaching. This is very important for two reasons: it gets them excited that they can receive the same results, and it positions you for

the next part, which is where you pitch your company.

3. Finally, position your service or product as a way they can achieve even greater results than they could if they were to follow your advice by themselves. Here is where you invite them to set up a meeting with you or with one of your sales executives.

The beauty of the free training is that it has two purposes: it serves as authority content, while at the same time setting you up in real time to make the sale. Free trainings should usually be held live, using webinar software such as GoToMeeting, Webex, Zoom, Google Hangouts or any other webinar platform.

You can also do it as a pre-recorded video training, with you or somebody from your company standing in front of a white board to illustrate the material you're teaching.

Video trainings using Facebook Live are increasing in popularity, and so far, there are no outsourcing providers from Latin America or the Caribbean using this approach to create content and to sell to prospects.

Finally, you can record the free training sessions and use them as evergreen content on your blog. You can also use it to generate leads by offering access to the video training when prospects give you their email address.

Authority content is a must-have in the arsenal of weapons nearshore providers must use to dominate in their market and achieve 10X the results of their competitors. It's what separates the serious companies from the also-rans.

4

THE RIGHT
WAY TO BUILD
YOUR WEBSITE

"The purpose of the homepage of a website is to get the visitor to page 2." – Marcus Sheridan

As we advance in this book, you'll start to see the logic of each sequence. After creating your piece of authority content, you will need a place from where you can offer your content. Today, that's your website – your home base on the web.

But what is the purpose of the website? Most companies get this wrong, and nearshore outsourcing companies are no exception. They approach their websites incorrectly, treating them as a place to inform visitors and potential clients all about their services. They describe what they do, list their services, and they even talk about the benefits and advantages of doing business with them instead of with some other outsourcing company or near shore company.

"What's wrong with that?" I hear you ask. "Shouldn't I be informing my market about what my services are?"

In a word, no.

The purpose of a website is to generate business. That's it! That's the one and only purpose of your website.

And the purpose of the website home page, according to Marcus Sheridan on his Sales Lion blog, is to get people to page two. If they get to page two, says Sheridan, "…they have expressed their interest. Now they've answered the classic retail question, 'Can I help you find what you're looking for?'"

Sheridan lists five classic mistakes most companies make when designing their website.

1. Using Sliders

Sheridan calls sliders "mankind's worst invention." Why? Because searchers today are looking to solve a problem quickly. When they come to your website, they want to find an answer to something they're looking for. All a slider does is slow them down and distract them from that purpose.

2. Headlines that Talk About Your Products

Another mistake is using headlines and website copy that

talk about your company, services and products. This is counter-intuitive, I know. But trust me (and Sheridan), on this. Customers don't care about you, or your business. They care about solving their own problem. That's why they're on your website in the first place. Your headlines and copy should talk about helping your customers solve a problem or help them get something they want.

Sheridan lists an example straight from the software world (I wonder why that is? Is it, maybe, because software companies are so notoriously bad at marketing?).

Compare these two headlines:

Offering Cloud Computing services globally. Fast. Reliable. Cost Effective.

vs.

Keep your company's records digitally backed up forever without experiencing downtime ever again. And save huge in the process.

Which is the best headline? Sheridan says the last one is the most effective, because it focuses on solving a major problem the potential customer is experiencing.

3. Talking About Company News

This is a pet peeve of mine, and I was glad Sheridan listed it. Nobody cares about your company's news: the company picnic they went on, the latest certification they obtained, or the award they won from SAP for being "partner of the year." Who cares about that?

Sheridan reminds us that we must continuously focus on our customers (the client pain gap as discussed in Chapter 1). Make customer-centricity central to the way we deliver our services, as we discussed in Chapter 2. Company news does not fulfill this rule.

4. Using Too Much Text

This is especially relevant to home page design. Leave all the text to second and third level pages. Use the "less is more" mantra for the home page. As Sheridan states, "Less is more. Less is more. Less is more." Your main goal is to help your customers find what they're looking for as quickly as possible. Too much text distracts them and confuses them.

5. Talking Too Much About Your Company

Thinking as a customer-centric company, whose goal is to help your clients close the gap between where they are now with where they want to be, you now know that talking too much about your company is a big no-no, especially on the home page. You can discuss it on the "About Us" page. But even then, talk about your company in a way that ties what you do with the problems you solve for your customers.

What's the right way to design a website, especially if you're a consulting or services company offering large dollar services? Turn your website into an "app."

Let me explain.

An app is the perfect metaphor for what a modern website should be, since it fulfills what your customers want to do. Your customers want to get something done. An app helps you get things done.

When people come to your website, they want to do something too: get answers to their questions and solve their problems.

SEO, Conversion, Content

SEO

So, you've learned that the purpose of your website is to generate business. But, there's one problem: your site will only generate business if people are able to find your site in the first place. That presents another problem. The traffic problem.

How are you going to drive traffic to your website? We discuss this in detail in Chapter 5, but let me touch on it a little bit here.

There are four main ways to generate traffic:

1. Organic Search
2. Organic Social
3. Public Relations (PR)
4. Paid Advertising

Let's touch briefly on the first one, organic search.

To get organic traffic you need to perform search engine optimization (SEO). Your website needs the elements necessary for Google and other search engines to find your site and recognize it for its authoritative content that it can show users whenever they type a query into the search bar.

There are many dimensions to SEO (which we'll discuss in a little more detail in Chapter 5). Technical SEO, such as your site's loading speed; navigability and technical errors; content, such as whether you publish authoritative content on certain topics; bounce rate, or whether your site pulls people into page two, as Marcus Sheridan says, and your backlink profile, or how many authoritative sites link to your website.

One of the key aspects to SEO is choosing a topic or a set of topics for which you'll optimize your site. By that, I mean choosing the keywords or keyphrases for optimization.

However, Google has been moving away from focusing on specific keywords, and instead is looking at user intent. When somebody searching on Google types something, they may not know (yet) what specific keyword or keyphrase will yield their best results. So, instead, Google has been focusing on salient entities, which are a grouping of similar keywords that reflect what the person intends to search for.

That depends on the themes or topics you want to find. When developing your website, you need to appeal to what your users are actually searching for, and that depends on how aware of their problem they are. Are they looking for answers to a problem, but don't know a solution, such as yours, exists? Or, are they actively searching for your product or service?

Conversion

Once you've driven traffic to your website, whether it's through organic search traffic, after you've optimized your site with proper SEO techniques, or you're driving a paid advertising campaign, then you need to focus on conversion.

What is conversion? Conversion is turning your visitors into prospects, turning your prospects into opportunities, and turning your opportunities into sales.

Your website needs to start by converting visitors into prospects. Another way to put this is to convert strangers into friends.

It's how to get your visitors past your home page into the second page, third page, or even the fourth page of your website.

Let's look back at the app metaphor. What is the purpose of an app on your mobile phone? To provide some kind of functionality so people can do something. People don't go to their Uber or Starbucks app to read about Uber or Starbucks. They go to these apps to get a ride or to order a coffee.

Your site needs to have the same effect. You need to convert visitors into users of your "app," which means you need them to *do something* when they get to your site. You need to get them involved, get them to take some type of action.

The best way to do that is to get them to download something of value that will help answer a burning question, or help them learn something so they can do their work better.

The most effective way to do that is to give them a way to become a customer right then and there.

Yes, that's right. Your goal should be to get relevant visitors to become your customer at that moment.

I know what you're thinking. Your services typically *start* at $20,000 for a smallish software development or BPO project. Your prospects can't make a split-second decision to spend $20,000 in one visit, right?

I'm not talking about convincing your website visitor to become a customer of your core offering right there and then. I'm asking you to get them to make a micro-commitment to your company. An impulse buy. Something that doesn't require them to get approval from anybody.

Let me use an analogy. McDonald's launched their famous Dollar Menu in 2002. You could get a double cheeseburger and other items for only a dollar each. Now, think about this. Anybody can spend a dollar without even blinking. If you want a snack, but don't want to go to the 7-11 to buy a chocolate bar or chips, just go to McDonald's and get a cheeseburger for a dollar.

But, when you get there, you decide you want some fries. And then you want a drink. And before you know it you've bought a whole meal.

The analogy is a stretch, I know, but hear me out here. What if you were to offer a micro-commitment that has the same psychological effect as turning your visitor into a customer, even though they haven't made the decision to spend $20,000 for you to build them an app?

What would that look like?

1. Sell a Book

What if you published a book and, on your website, you offered the book for one dollar? Who wouldn't pay a dollar for a book? You could offer a physical book, sell the book for a dollar, and then charge your visitor a minimal shipping fee. This is similar to what Accelerance did with their book, *Software Without Borders.*

2. Offer a Free Training

You could also offer free training, such as "How to Digitally Transform Your Business." This could be delivered as a live webinar. Now, even though it's free (by registering for the training you're not actually becoming a client), but if your prospect attends the training, they're committing actual time to your company. Time is more valuable than money in most cases. Someone who dedicates an hour or two to attend one of your training sessions has just invested valuable time getting convinced to your way of thinking. They have become a "customer" in their mind.

3. Offer a Low Cost or Free Strategy Session

Offer a form on your website from which your prospects can schedule a low-cost or a free strategy session. The strategy session can be a one-on-one Skype or GoToMeeting session, or it can be an in-person session, where you get into the details of your customer's business to create a strategic roadmap or a proof of concept.

You could create a beautiful front-end "app mockup." Your team could create this, using HTML5 that emulates what a real app would look like, but without the back-end integrations. It would take one UX/UI expert on your team a couple of days to produce. Or you could create a business process workflow if you're offering BPO services.

You get the picture.

In each of these cases your prospect has made an impulse decision to make a micro-commitment to your company, and what they get is something very valuable.

The excitement a realistic mockup can create can help you close your prospect on your core services. Can you imagine the look on the face of an insurance company executive when he or she sees a mockup of a self-service insurance app that looks and feels real?

They can touch it, feel it, they can visualize their customers using this application. In their mind they have already become your customer.

No website should ever be without a way for your visitors to become immediate customers.

One caveat. If you're offering a free strategy session you need to thoroughly qualify your prospects. You don't want to commit valuable developer resources to creating an intricate working mock-up for a startup with no money. Make sure your online form asks some serious questions about company size, the role of the person within the company, and what their goals are. Make sure you emphasize they need to enter a corporate email address, not a Gmail or Yahoo address.

Tell them How to do Business with You

What if your prospects know exactly what they want, and they want to hire a company right away? Your website should be ready to handle hot prospects who are ready to buy. Do this by teaching them exactly how to do business with you.

Describe your process for getting started, and make the getting started process easy. If your process starts by scheduling a customer interview to understand their current situation and their goals, explain how you conduct those interviews. Publish your phone number so they can call you right away. Better yet, provide a contact form on every page (put it on the sidebar of each page that describes your services).

My recommendation is to use a contact form that generates an automatic call from your company to your prospect. If all you provide is a "contact us" form – which generates an email to your sales department – answer that email **within an hour or less** to improve your chances of closing the deal.

Why is it important to your potential customers that you describe how to do business with you? Two reasons:

> 1. Prospects typically don't know what to do or how to do it. Most have never contracted outsourcing services before. By telling them

exactly what to do, you're taking them gently by the hand and setting yourself up as the trusted expert.

2. When visitors come to your website, they are looking for somebody to tell them what to do. When you tell them what to do, tell them to do it right now. Say "Pick up the phone and call us at 347-555-5555." Telling them what to do satisfies an urge they have that hasn't been satisfied by other websites.

Explain How Your Process Works

One of the most valuable psychological tricks you can do is to get your visitors to imagine what it's like to do business with you. There are two ways to do that: through case studies, and by describing your process.

Let me explain the importance of describing your process, and how to do it.

Create a page on your website describing how you will work with the prospect on every project. One of the big unanswered questions your prospects have when landing on your website is: "What will it be like to work with this company?"

Describing the process answers that question. It gets them to imagine what it's like to work with you. If you follow a unique methodology, describe that. Also, describe the client onboarding process, how often you will be in contact, whether you will schedule regular weekly or daily calls with them, and how much of their time and effort you will require.

The last part is very important. Not only are they hiring you to do some work, but they know they need to be involved in the process. Their days are very busy, so knowing how much of their day-to-day they need to put in helps answer an important objection.

Be Completely Transparent

Finally, you need to be transparent. One of the biggest errors I see on the websites of many Latin American outsourcing providers is the absence of the names of executives and team members.

However, I have seen this changing. Many newer outsourcing companies share the photos and profiles of not just their executive team members, but all their developers or customer service reps (CSRs). They even share photos of office parties and company events.

This can also be taken a little too far. Posting content about your company's Halloween party, or about how committed your people are to their jobs, is still talking about you and your company. It doesn't talk to what you provide your customers, or the transformation you provide.

The type of transparency that works best is when you talk about your company, emphasizing the transformation you provide to your clients. Let me give you an example.

On your blog, you might discuss a new software development hack one of your developers discovered, and how this could benefit your company, or you might describe something you achieved for a client and the positive results they had because of it.

If you ever blog about your team-building retreat, don't just talk about the retreat, talk about the five lessons you learned at the retreat that will help your customers.

The bottom line is, your website needs to sell your services. Make sure it's easy for Google to serve up your website to people looking for the services you offer. Treat your site like an app so they can do something useful, like make a micro-commitment to become your client right away. Explain how to start doing business with your company. Help them visualize what it's like to work with you by describing your processes.

Finally, be transparent. Share what your company does – but make it valuable to your clients.

5

HOW TO DRIVE TRAFFIC TO YOUR WEBSITE

"He who can spend the most to acquire a customer, wins . . ." – Ryan Deiss

We've discussed getting your website right. But your website won't serve you at all if there is no traffic coming to it. The good news is, traffic is in abundant supply; you just have to know how to divert some of that traffic to your website.

There are four main categories of traffic: paid, earned, organic, and owned.

With paid traffic you're tapping into already existing traffic that other media entities and websites control. The most common here are Facebook, Google, and LinkedIn. But, this also refers to advertising on other sites that have niche traffic in your market space.

Owned traffic is traffic that you own, and it refers primarily to your mailing list. We don't include your website or social media properties here, because you don't necessarily own this traffic, but it is traffic you control. We'll discuss the details below.

Then there's organic traffic, which we described in the previous chapter. This includes organic search and organic social.

Finally, there's earned traffic. The most common forms of earned traffic are PR and guest blogging.

Paid Traffic

Paid traffic is the way to get traffic quickly to your website. It's also the most expensive. In the age of social media and content marketing, marketing gurus have tended to dismiss paid traffic as not truly legitimate. Their argument is, if you're any good at social media and content creation, why would you need to pay for traffic?

Well, there are three great reasons to drive paid traffic to your site.

1. Paid Traffic Is Immediate

The startup community has popularized the minimum viable product (MVP) concept. By creating a minimum viable product – either a product with the minimum number of features that allow you to offer something of value to a client, or maybe even just a sales page to gauge interest – you're getting quick feedback from the market about what customers will pay for. It's either fast fail, or fast success. With the MVP, you avoid long development cycles that last months or even years, only to find out that nobody wants what you're selling.

Paid traffic can help you apply MVP principles to your landing pages, website, and offers. Paid traffic is like a faucet you can turn on and turn off at will. It allows you to drive visitors to your landing page or website, and get immediate feedback. Instead of waiting months for a page to rank on Google for certain search terms, you can find out today whether your page will convert customers.

2. It Allows You to Leapfrog the Competition

In the quote at the beginning of this chapter, marketing thought leader Ryan Deiss declared an age-old truth: "He who can spend the most to acquire a customer, wins." Ryan Deiss actually got this from marketing legend, Dan Kennedy. In fact, Dan Kennedy made the explicit argument that you might even have to lose money on the first sale, but the payoff is that you beat your competition. He says, " . . . the marketer with the willingness and ability to invest in acquiring customers, even losing money on the first sale AND with an effective strategy for maximizing customer value, has an enormous competitive advantage."

Kennedy recognized that business owners would have a difficult time accepting this message, because it's counterintuitive. But, think about this. If you are willing to lose money on an initial sale because of how much you were willing to spend on advertising, then maximize the value you provide by upselling and cross-selling, you can far exceed the results any of your competitors can achieve.

3. You Can Target Customers with Pinpoint Precision

Despite complaints that platforms like Google and Facebook have become "big brother," tracking your every move and documenting your tastes, habits, and who you hang out with, the benefits to marketers are incredible.

Today, with Facebook advertising, for example, you not only can target specific audiences according to demographics, title, geography, age, gender and marital status, but you can target them by intent. For example, you can create a custom audience to advertise to, based on other pages they've liked and groups they're members of. You can advertise to your competitor's customers and prospects, the people most likely to respond positively to your message.

Earned Traffic

Earned traffic is one of the most powerful types of traffic you could get coming to your site. It's the fancy name for PR. It's when a blog with hundreds of thousands of readers, or a news site, or an influencer, mentions you.

There are three benefits to earned traffic: 1. The audience is already pre-disposed to react favorably to your offer; 2. It's more likely to be the right audience for your brand; 3. It taps into the trust generated by the authority of an already prestigious and popular destination.

1. Audience Is Pre-Disposed Towards Your Offer

When an authoritative industry publication or news site like Forbes or CIO.com, or a blog with hundreds of thousands of subscribers, publishes an article about you, the traffic it sends to you already has a favorable opinion about your company. The site has conferred its authority to you when sending you the traffic. Visitors who come to you from one of these published articles are much more likely to subscribe to your content, contact your company, or contract your services.

In a case study mentioned in the book, *The Content Promotion Manifesto* by Chad Pollitt, an article appearing on a major media publication about the company in question boosted conversions on their website. The lead count went up 82 percent in the month the article was published compared to the prior month. Previous to the article being published, their site-wide conversion rate was only 3.9% from existing traffic. With the new traffic coming to the company's website from the article, site-wide conversions grew to 9.4 percent, with the highest day bringing in 19.9 percent.

2. The Audience Is More Likely to be the Right Audience

If an article about your company, or an interview with you, is published on a major media publication, more than likely that publication is going to already have an audience that is aligned with your company. If you're a software development company, an article about you in *Information Week* will bring IT managers, Directors of Engineering, and CIOs.

3. You Borrow the Trust of the Publication

Closely related to #1 above, traffic coming to you from earned media has a high level of trust. It's a fundamental human psychological characteristic: we're more likely to trust something when it comes from a third party than when we talk about ourselves. It's why testimonials are so powerful. It's why reviews on sites like Yelp are so valuable. It's why referrals are more likely to turn into sales than cold prospects.

When a trusted source, like your best friend, or your favorite news publication, recommends your company, the person who comes to you already has a high level of trust about your company.

Organic Traffic

Organic traffic is what search engines or your social media channels send you. They're both organic, but they're different.

1. Organic Search Engine Traffic

Organic search traffic is intent-based traffic. People are searching for answers to very specific questions on Google, Bing or Yahoo.

Google, which controls 75% of the search market, has one goal when it comes to search: " . . . to provide the best results possible to your query." As a result, Google's search bots scout the web looking for the best content to answer its users' billions of questions. As a company with a website, you need to help Google find your useful content and answer the burning questions on your prospects' minds. Organize the content on your site so it's useful, easy to understand, and comprehensive.

Google looks at the quality of your content. It also looks at the signals that more authoritative sites send about your content. If your content is good, then an authoritative site might link to a page on your site. This is a "yes" vote in your favor, telling Google that your content is relevant and valuable.

But Google also emphasizes your UX. It's not enough to publish high quality information. Your site must be easy to use, easy to understand, and fast. Google looks at your site's load speed, and will demote sites that take too long to load.

With Google's "mobilegeddon" algorithm update of April 2015, if your site isn't mobile friendly, it will also get demoted.

Finally, Google actively tries to eliminate low-quality content from its search engine results pages (SERPs). This can be content that is too short, poorly written, or not relevant.

So how do you drive higher organic traffic to your site?

Focus on publishing high quality content that provides value to your audience. Value means content that is relevant, educational, informative, comprehensive, thorough, easy-to-consume, and visual.

In his article *Google's 200 Ranking Factors: The Complete List* (this post is an example of the kind of content Google loves), Brian Dean provides a comprehensive overview of what Google takes into consideration when prioritizing websites and pages.

What really stands out on this list is that the longer the content, the better. This is very counter-intuitive. Most of us assume that shorter content is better. We think, "People don't read, so we need to write 300 or 400-word blog posts."

Most nearshore outsourcing companies make the "short content is better" mistake. They tend to publish shorter articles on their blogs. This error isn't limited to smaller nearshore companies. Even the largest nearshore outsourcing providers tend to publish shorter content! But, these articles are not very valuable, at least according to Google. In research conducted by SerpIQ, they found that the longer the content, the higher in the SERPs the content appeared.

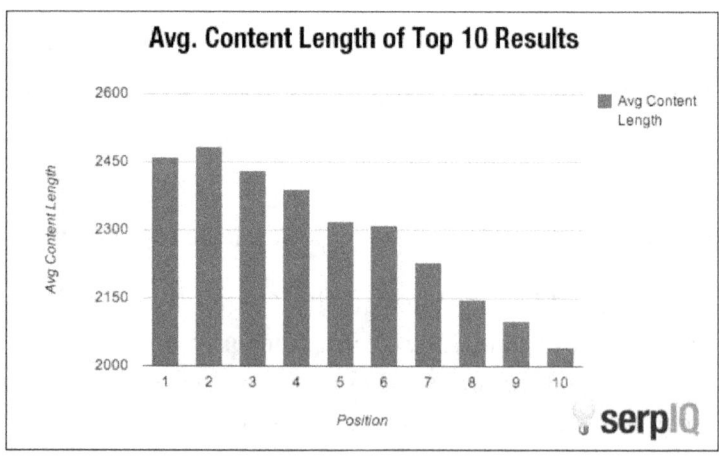

Source: 2 SerpIQ

2. Organic Social Media Traffic

According to Michael Stelzner, CEO of Social Media Examiner, organic social media traffic is dead. In fact, in an interview with the hosts of the *Perpetual Traffic* podcast, Stelzner says that only 4% of the traffic to his site – the most important site on the topic of social media – comes from organic social media!

Stelzner said that people do share content on Facebook, Twitter, and LinkedIn, but, typically, they share it to look good to their peers. Most people don't read the content shared on social media.

I would not recommend using organic social media as a strategy to drive traffic to your website. Social media is better used as an engagement tool with current clients, or as a customer service platform.

If you focus on Facebook, Stelzner recommends using Facebook Live video, not as a way to drive traffic to your website, but as a way to build a responsive community within Facebook.

Owned Traffic

Owned traffic refers to your subscribers – and this means email. In a world of social media, email is more relevant than ever. In fact, email is so important that Social Media Examiner has made getting subscribers to their email newsletter their number one goal!

Owned traffic is the best traffic you can get. Subscribers to your email list have given you permission to send them content, and the occasional commercial message. By subscribing to you, they have made a small commitment towards your company that takes them closer to becoming an actual customer than somebody who arrives as cold traffic to your website.

Getting subscribers is the best way to continue to feed people your blog content every time you publish something new. It's also the best way to sell to them. I'll get into more detail in Chapter 7, when I discuss "Escalation."

The most important benefit of owned traffic is that you have your own audience. You don't have to rely on Google organic results and its ever-changing search algorithm. You don't have to rely on organic social traffic, and its diminishing effectiveness. You don't have to rely on the constant investment into paid traffic. And, you don't have to rely on the constant PR hustle to get major media properties to write about you.

Owned traffic is really the end goal of all the other forms of traffic mentioned here. Paid, earned, and organic traffic should lead to owned traffic, which means building your own audience, which means building your subscriber base.

That means you should act like your own media company. The internet has leveled the playing field, and has made it possible for every company to become its own media company.

What is central to the business model of media companies? That's right: subscribers!

I'll end this chapter with the sage words of digital marketing guru Gary Vaynerchuk:

> "Whether you like it or not, every person is now a media company. The tools are easy, free, and everywhere. More importantly, producing content is now the BASELINE for all brands and companies. It literally doesn't matter what business you're in, what industry you operate in, if you're not producing content, you basically don't exist. So, what's your excuse?"

6

SELLING 2.0:
HOW TO REACH
THE RIGHT
CUSTOMERS

"The foundational root of all success in sales is a fanatical focus on prospecting," — Jeb Blount

In previous chapters, we've focused on digital marketing. We live in a world dominated by the Internet where Facebook has two billion users – twice the size of China! But nearshore outsourcers don't have a massive audience. Because your services are considered a big-ticket B2B item, you have a limited addressable market.

It makes no sense to wait for inbound marketing to bring

you clients that may or may not be a right fit for your company. You need to use good old-fashioned outbound marketing, but with a modern twist.

In his groundbreaking book, *How to Get a Meeting With Anyone*, author Stu Heinecke lays out the strategies today's B2B companies are using to reach out directly to your "Top 100" list.

Prospecting and Your Top 100 List

Heinecke describes an exciting possibility for companies who execute a well thought-out "contact campaign" (contact campaign is his term for outbound marketing). Heinecke says that a well-executed contact campaign can turn you into a " . . . connected, powerful person, a VIP . . . "

And the key to that, according to Heinecke, is to identify and define your Top 100. "There is a small group of people who, if they become your clients or strategic partners, will transform the scale of your business."

Who are your top 100 target customers? They are your dream clients, the clients who will transform your business by their ability to attract other clients. They are typically well-known brands in their industry, they have large budgets, and can introduce you to other departments or other companies.

Types of Contact Campaigns

Contact campaigns, according to Heinecke, are sales-oriented direct marketing campaigns on steroids. They are outbound, focused marketing initiatives designed to either support the sales process, or to directly generate sales.

Depending on your comfort level with contacting clients directly, you can choose any of the following types of contact campaigns to reach your Top 100

Phone Calls

In a post I wrote in 2009, I predicted the death of telemarketing. In a world of voicemail, social media, and text messaging, who would think of telemarketing any longer?

Actually, cold-calling is coming back – but with a twist. In a recent podcast hosted by Jason Swenk, guest Gene Hammett, a business leader, speaker, strategic coach, and sales pro, talks about the 100-call challenge.

The 100-call challenge is a two-week sprint where you commit to having *100 conversations*, not just 100 dials. Hammett's goal during one particular 100-call challenge was to get more clients and to get speaking engagements.

Let's look more closely at his efforts to get more clients.

Hammett divided his efforts across two types of prospects: lost deals and new clients. With lost deals he pulled a list of previous prospects who had told him "no" at some point in time. But, instead of just making a "check-in" call, he took a strategic approach. He remembered exactly the topic of the last conversation he had with each prospect, and used the call as an opportunity to follow-up on that topic.

For example, if a previous prospect told you he wanted to reduce his customer service costs by 10% through an automated self-service app, but for some reason they decided to build it themselves, you could ask the prospect, "How is that app coming along? Were you able to successfully build it and reduce customer service costs by 10%?"

That might be the exact question that could re-engage your lost prospect and convince them to try your services.

To approach new clients, Hammett devised a strategic approach. Instead of calling to ask for an appointment, which could be a major turn-off to cold prospects who don't want to talk to another sales person, he adopted the "content marketing" mindset by offering value up front. He decided to give something away before asking for something in return.

Hammett decided to organize a series of exclusive events, limiting attendance to about eight CEOs or high-level executives. These were either a cocktail hour or a catered workshop. During these executive events he would deliver free information in the form of an executive briefing.

Then Hammett hired a virtual assistant to assemble a list of 500 CEOs of high profile companies he wanted to contact. He set out to get them on the phone, using emails and voice mails to connect with the executives. It took a while to get the target CEOs on the phone, but he connected with several of them and filled his executive briefings.

The result? Hammett got three new clients through his two-week 100-call challenge!

Direct Mail on Steroids

Another tactic coming back into vogue? Direct mail. But for B2B contact campaigns, I recommend direct mail on steroids. Let me explain.

Consider sending something that really stands out – from the appearance of the package or envelope, to the innovative contents of the mailing.

In his book, Heinecke describes the brilliant campaign tech startup NoWait executed. NoWait offers an app for restaurants to help their patrons avoid the annoying long wait times during popular dining hours.

NoWait sent iPads preloaded with a personalized video addressed to each restaurant executive.

Here's a full excerpt from Heinecke's book describing the campaign:

> "Every unit arrived in the original Apple packaging, but with a few alterations. The tiny instructions booklet was replaced with a NoWait mini brochure, and the protective screen sheet was replaced with a sheet of instructions: Step 1, turn it on; Step 2, tap the NoWait video icon.

> "What awaited was a video, individually shot just for each target executive. It started with hidden lapel-cam footage, clearly showing the "interviewer's" point of view, walking up to one of their restaurants, then into the overcrowded waiting space within. When the interviewer finally reached the

reservations desk, he was told it would be an hour-long wait.

"The interviewer continued, engaging in conversations around the room, asking how patrons felt about waiting so long for a table. Then the video switched to a segment introducing the NoWait app, and explaining how it does away with annoyingly long waits. It was a beautiful delivery of the company's value proposition, using slick video production to present it in a fashion no sales rep could match in person. The video concluded with a segment showing the NoWait CEO speaking directly to the target executive, telling them how he loves eating at their restaurants, but hates having to wait an hour for a table. He then invites the target executive to connect with them and put the app to the test."

There are other ways to execute the "direct mail on steroids" concept. You can FedEx a letter with a gift inside so it's a 3D package and not just a flat letter.

Or, if you decided to write a book like I suggested in Chapter 3, you could send a copy of your book to your prospects.

Video Emails

If you want to stay with digital, you can always send direct, personalized emails to your prospects. But, don't just send the standard email that everybody sends. Those emails get ignored and sent to the spam folder. Instead, send a personalized video to your prospects.

I recommend using a tool like Covideo to produce and send personalized private videos. Write a short, personalized introduction in the email telling your prospect what you're sending and how the video can help them.

Finally, offer something of value in the video message itself. Teach something, invite them to download a report or eBook from your site, or invite them to an executive briefing or webinar.

I recommend picking up a copy of Stu Heinecke's book to get a complete overview of how to execute a contact campaign.

The Emergence of Virtual Selling

But by far the most important development in outbound selling, and enterprise selling in general, is the emergency of Virtual Selling. In their book *Next Era Selling*, authors Anneke Seley and Britton Manasco describe the emergences of a new type of selling particular to the North American market. It's a complete contrast to how big tickets sales are conducted in Latin American countries.

A friend of mine was describing, for example, how difficult it was to manage his Mexico City-based company from his new home in Austin, TX. He said that despite his best efforts to sell new product offerings by phone to his regular clients, they always told him: "When are you coming to Mexico? We need to have lunch and I want you to come to my office to present your new offering to me in person."

Not so in the U.S. market. Manasco and Seley describe

the *Virtual Selling Imperative,* which can be divided into five strategies:

1. Front Office Fusion

Companies are unifying and aligning the front office (sales, marketing, professional services and customer care/success), and spanning silos that might have otherwise led to band handoffs and poor service. They're actively collaborating to deliver exceptional customer experience every time.

2. The Inside Upside

Companies are also raising the ceilings and lowering the walls that used to confine insides sales teams. They've liberated them to expand their territories and coverage areas, and have raised quota sizes and average deal sizes.

3. The Outside Upside

Companies are also encouraging field or outside reps to act in more consultative ways, going deeper within accounts, narrowing their funnels and reducing the number of accounts they handle.

4. The Inside-Outside Alliance

With the alliance of inside and outside sales teams, companies can expand their coverage and coordinate deals more efficiently, while bringing more professionalism to their sales approach.

5. Networked Specialization

Buyers now seek more guidance and support, pushing firms to develop specialists with expertise to help clients with their particular needs. Enterprise clients have an average of five team members to help decide on purchasing or contracting decisions. The best response by nearshore service providers is to deploy specialists to meet the needs of these decision stakeholders.

Co-author Manasco told me: "With a good list, your own Zoom.us account, a great PowerPoint, and good selling skills, you can close a lot more deals from your office than when you're out on the road."

U.S. buyers don't want to meet with sellers anymore. The cost of traveling to visit clients in different cities is cost-prohibitive. It seems that everybody wants to engage in a virtual sales model.

This is revolutionary for nearshore service providers. You can now sell your services from the comfort of your office in Guadalajara or Lima, instead of investing in monthly trips to the U.S. or expensive office space in San Mateo, California.

The Return of Phone Prospecting

I got my start in high-tech sales and marketing doing old-school cold calling. I worked for a call center where my job was to call into a database of Fortune 2000 IT managers, database administrators, directors of IT and CIOs to generate leads on behalf of our customers (companies such as Cisco, 3Com, Amdahl, Business Objects).

It wasn't unusual for me to make up to 80 calls a day. It was brutal work. People would hang up on me, tell me they weren't interested, and not return my calls.

But I was good at it.

I was quickly promoted to the business development side of the house. My job was to sell call center services to the CMOs, VPs of Marketing, VPs of Sales and CEOs of high-tech companies. I called on established companies as well as startups.

Our services cost anywhere from $10,000 a month to $120,000 a month or more. These sales were 95% over the phone. I never visited a client – they came to visit us. In fact, if I could convince the executive team of an up-and-coming high tech company to visit our state-of-the-art call center, I was virtually guaranteed to close the sale.

Each company had to pay the first quarter's fee up front. It wasn't uncommon for me to receive a $50,000 check for the first three months of a project.

Every time we got a check in, my sales manager would make us go from desk to desk showing it off to my fellow sales colleagues. It was a real hard-core sales environment. It was reminiscent of movie *The Wolf of Wall Street*. This scene of Leonardo Di Caprio closing his first sale over the phone was eerily similar to our sales environment.

Wolf of Wall Street with Leonardo Di Caprio

You can watch the video here: https://youtu.be/ RauYoB0I9q4

Except we weren't selling fraudulent stocks – we were selling very effective, aggressive, outbound lead generation services.

I was regularly one of the top three sales reps each month. Everybody on the sales team knew where everybody else stood. The sales managers installed a leader board on the main wall of the sales floor with the names of all 10 "sales dogs" (as they called us), with our position and sales for the month. There was no doubt who was at the top of the list, and who was at the bottom. Talk about peer pressure!

I was good. Very good. But that was the mid to late 1990s, and the internet was just starting to become a major factor in sales and marketing.

Fast-forward to 2007, about a decade later. I was on the sales team at a software company that sold data integration applications to mid-sized companies. I thought, "This is going to be a piece of cake. I'm just going to use my usual bag of phone tricks and close tons of deals."

Except it didn't happen. Nobody answered their phones. Nobody returned my calls. My pipeline was close to empty. That was around the same time I started blogging, thank God. If I hadn't picked up my new content marketing skill, I'd probably be a barista at Starbucks right now (not to knock on Starbucks baristas – they're some of my favorite people!).

It seemed like cold calling had died a sudden death, and the killer was technology. Voicemail. Email. Smartphones. Text messaging.

I even wrote about the death of cold calling in my first blog as an independent consultant. I received a lot of comments and emails as a result of that post, mostly from phone reps in Spanish-speaking countries asking for advice about what they could do now that cold calling was dead!

Now I feel guilty about writing that article, because cold calling is back. With a vengeance.

In his book *Fanatical Prospecting*, Jeb Blount declares triumphantly: "The statistics don't lie. We see between a 15 percent and 80 percent contact rate on the phones depending on the industry, product, and role level of the contact."

Blount says that teleprospecting, the politically correct term for cold calling, gets higher response rates than email, and is "light years" higher than social prospecting!

Blount again:

"It gets better. We have stats on phone prospecting going back to the early 1990s, and we are seeing clear trends that contact rates via phone have actually risen by around 5 percentage points. We don't know the exact reason why more prospects are answering their phones, but we suspect three drivers:

1. **Phones are anchored to people, not desks**. It is common for prospects to answer their mobile phone when you call them – either because their mobile line is their only line or because their office line rolls over to their mobile line.

2. **No one is calling**. Because so much sales communication has shifted to e-mail, social inboxes, and text, phones are not ringing nearly as much as in the past. Because of this, salespeople who call are standing out in the crowd and getting through.

3. **Prospects are getting burned out on impersonal, irrelevant (and often automated) prospecting e-mails.** E-mail and social inboxes are being flooded with crap. Prospects are hungry for something different – a live, authentic human being."

The Teleprospecting Formula

Blount provides an effective formula for teleprospecting in today's environment:

Block Out a Teleprospecting Power Hour

Have you heard of Parkinson's Law? Blount describes it as the theory that "...work tends to expand to fill the time allotted for it." You can see this law in operation in sales departments all over the world. Most sales people are allergic to phones, and if you tell them to pick up the phone to start prospecting, they'll never do it. Or maybe they'll make a few calls a day, and that's it.

When their sales manager asks them: "What have you done all day?" They'll often respond: "I've been entering my sales notes in the CRM system." Or: "I'm filling out my expense report." Or even: "I'm working on a proposal for the hot prospect I just spoke to."

But these are all excuses. When your sales people don't block out a specific chunk of time to teleprospect, they'll end up frittering their time away in busy work. Playing with the CRM, filling out expense reports, and working on proposals are just excuses that keep sales people from making phone calls.

Blount also describes *Horstman's Corollary* to Parkinson's Law. This is the opposite of what I just described. Blount says that work will contract to fit into the time allowed. For example, if you schedule an hour of phone calls each day and instruct your sales people to make at least 25 phone calls within that hour, they'll magically do it! All of a sudden they become super productive, hyper-focused sales machines.

Blount's firm, Sales Gravy, calls these Power Hours. A Power Hour is a one-hour (or even a half hour) time block designated for nothing but teleprospecting. No emails. No social media. No texting. No distractions. Just an hour of pure, solid phone prospecting.

There is something powerful in concentrating a ton of sales power into a focused and limited amount of time. It's similar to using a magnifying glass to concentrate the power of the sun on a pinpoint area. You can set a piece of paper on fire with the focused power of the sun.

And you can you can set your sales on fire with a focused hour of phone prospecting.

I've recently started teleprospecting again, and I've been

pleasantly surprised by the results! Blount is right. It's amazing how many people will answer their phones, and how quickly I've accelerated my sales pipeline by doing something that most other sales people are afraid of doing.

The Five Step Teleprospecting Framework

Blount recommends following a simple, direct, no-nonsense five-step cold-calling process:

1. Get Their Attention

When you get somebody on the phone, address your prospect immediately by their name. There's no sound sweeter than the sound of your own name. Your prospects will react more positively when you use their name than if you just launch into a script. Start with, "Hi John…" or "Hi Rebecca…"

2. Identify Yourself

Immediately announce who you are. Prospect don't like it when an anonymous person launches into a sales script without identifying themselves. When you say your name, it disarms your prospects and makes you sound legitimate. Say: "Hi Rebecca, this is Fernando Labastida from Nearshore Marketing…"

3. Tell Them The Reason For Your Call

When selling nearshore services, your number one goal for making a cold-call is to schedule a phone appointment. Don't try to tell them about your services over the phone! Come right out and say: "The reason for my call is to set up an appointment with you."

4. Build a Bridge to the Why

Your prospects want to know why they should set up an appointment with you, so give them a reason. One of the most powerful words in the art of persuasion is the word *because*. Robert Cialdini, in his famous book, *Influence: The Psychology of Persuasion*, says:

> "A well-known principle of human behavior says that when we ask someone to do us a favor we will be more successful if we provide a reason. People simply like to have reasons for what they do."

When you say "because," you're more likely to get people to agree to a phone appointment with you. You could give them a 'because' by saying something like: "A lot of companies we talk to want to implement digital transformation in their companies, but they're confused about how to start. We've been helping companies successfully build a roadmap to their digital transformation, and I'd like to share some of the highlights of our methodology with you..."

5. Ask For The Appointment

Once you give your prospects the 'because,' then ask for the appointment. Blount's recommendation is to already have a couple of days and times ready. You want your prospects to know that you're busy, and that you only have a few times available. If you say: "When would be a good time for you? I'm wide open this week...," you sound weak and desperate.

There's no space in this book to go into full detail on the fanatical prospecting methodology. I recommend you read Blount's book, which you can purchase here.

7

HOW TO CLOSE MORE SALES WITH THE ESCALATION MODEL

Now that we've come this far, let's discuss how to sell your service. You've created your authority content, you've generated paid, earned, organic, and owned traffic, and you've executed your contact campaigns. What do you do when you finally have a prospect you can talk to?

That's what this chapter is about.

The Traditional vs. the Escalation Model

The standard way you're probably used to selling your service is to pitch your full service – whether it's a development project, staff augmentation service, or a monthly BPO retainer. Your sales process probably looks like this: a phone call, a meeting, another phone call, you send a proposal for your core service, and then you make several follow-up calls or send follow-up email, and then you hear nothing back from your prospect.

The traditional model is broken. But, it's the way it's always been done, and the only way you've ever heard of doing it.

I would like to introduce the "escalation method." It consists of a few additional steps before selling your core offering, but it has the effect of increasing the percentage of prospects who buy your core offering.

What is the escalation method? You offer your prospects a smaller, less expensive initial offering that lowers the barrier to entry of becoming a client. Then you upgrade them to your core service, or maybe an intermediary offering. Finally, you escalate them to your core offering.

The success of this method can be attributed to the core psychological principles outlined in the book, *Influence: The Psychology of Persuasion* by Robert Cialdini. In his book, Cialdini discusses six psychological elements of marketing designed to persuade people to do what you want them to do.

One of them is *reciprocity.* Reciprocity leverages the power of giving something to somebody before asking them for something in return. This creates a sense of obligation with the recipient, especially if what you've given to them is really valuable or useful to your prospect.

For example, offering a free executive briefing, as I described in the previous chapter, is a type of reciprocity offer. Sending somebody a copy of your book, or offering a free eBook or report as a download, are other types of reciprocity.

Cialdini also introduces the concept of *commitment and consistency*. Cialdini says that once somebody has taken action on something, the natural human tendency is to try to be consistent with this initial action.

So, for example, if you offer a small taste or version of your service at a very low cost, it's much easier for your prospect to say "yes." It's an impulse buy. Your prospect doesn't have to seek budgetary approval for something this small.

But, once they make the first small purchase, and they experience this small "taste" of your service, they're much more likely to buy something from you in the future. Why? Because in their mind, they have become a customer. They paid you money, even if it was a nominal amount. They now want to stay consistent with that initial tiny commitment. It's now a psychological need for them.

Finally, Cialdini talks about *authority*. I mention authority in Chapter 3. In addition to publishing content that establishes you as an authority in your field, when you offer a lower-cost item and deliver something of awesome value, you are also establishing authority. The authority comes from the value, and from the fact that they spent money on something you produced.

The Elements of the Escalation Method

The escalation method is not just a marketing and sales strategy –it's a solid business strategy. Ryan Deiss, in his article Customer Value Optimization – his version of the escalation method – says it's the system that McDonald's, Starbucks, Best Buy, Beach Body (makers of the PX90 workout), and *Sports Illustrated* have used to dominate their markets and become household names.

The "Before" and "After"

I discussed this in Chapter 1, "Selling Your Transformation – Not Your Service." You need to determine what your customers have (or don't have) now, and what they'll have after they acquire your product or service. But don't stop at the "not have" and "have." If you want to really excel at marketing, focus on the feelings, the status, the average day, and the enemy your customers are battling as it relates to the "before" and "after."

If you can nail down the deeper aspects of the "before" and "after," you can charge more, create more loyalty, elicit passion and desire, and write excellent marketing copy. If you can identify what a customer feels "before" and "after" they get the transformation your service provides, it then becomes easy to come up with the right words to use in any advertising, landing pages, or blog posts you publish.

For example, if you know that Directors of Development of mid-sized regional banks in the United States are *frustrated* because they can't find the talent to build a self-service bank account management app, then you can use that *frustration* in any advertising offer or landing page you write promoting your outsourced development services aimed at regional banks.

Your Traffic Source

Ryan Deiss says companies don't have a traffic problem. Instead, companies might have a business model problem, an offer problem, or a measurement problem. If you have the right process in place, traffic is not a problem. According to Deiss:

> "What if I told you that every time you get a visitor to a web page you make $10 in profit? Could you get traffic to that web page? Heck yes you could. You could pay up to $10 to get a visitor to that web page and still break even. In fact, you'll be able to pay more than $10 to get a visitor to that page when you truly understand the whole of Customer Value Optimization."

Once you're able to get your escalation method right, then getting traffic to your website should be no problem. Then, you can afford to spend as much as you can to get more traffic, because you know you'll be profitable with the traffic you get.

Renowned marketer, Dan Kennedy said, "Ultimately, the business that can spend the most to acquire a customer wins." You just have to have the right escalation method in place when you bring that traffic.

How do you get that traffic? Through paid traffic, earned traffic, organic traffic, and owned traffic, as we discuss in Chapter 5:

Lead Magnet

Ryan Deiss likes to compare the escalation method with the dating process. He said that establishing a relationship with new customers is like dating.

The lead magnet is can be compared to the beginning of the dating process, but with potential customers.

Deiss says when you start a relationship with a member of the opposite sex, you don't ask him or her to get married (or to go to bed with you) the moment you meet them at a party or at a nightclub. If you're a man, the woman will slap you in the face. If you're a woman, the man will probably run away.

There is a logical process you go through when starting a relationship with somebody who might one day become your spouse. You meet for the first time, then you meet for coffee, then you might meet for dinner or a movie. Then you might go hiking, and you might start a physical relationship. Eventually you'll meet the parents. Once you meet the parents, then the next logical step is to ask for your significant other's hand in marriage.

The same goes for business relationships. If you try to ask your client to buy your core offering from you right away, it's like asking somebody you just met at a party to marry you.

They don't know you, they don't trust you, and they don't even like you, yet.

So how do you initiate a business relationship? You need to get them to like you first. If you meet somebody at a party, you tell good stories. You ask them to dance with you. You tell jokes.

In business, the way to get a prospect to like you is to engage them with a piece of authority content, like I mentioned in Chapter 3.

Going back to the dating analogy, if you liked each other after the party, you might want to invite the person to go on a coffee date with you. In business the equivalent of that is to offer a lead magnet.

What is a lead magnet?

Ryan Deiss again tells us, "The Lead Magnet is an irresistible bribe that gives a specific chunk of value to a prospect in exchange for their contact information."

This is usually in the form of a free download, like a PDF, that you give to somebody after they fill out a form. They haven't bought anything from you, yet, but they are giving up something else of value: their email address.

This triggers Cialdini's *commitment and consistency* effect.

The best type of lead magnet is something specific. Instead of offering an eBook on *How to Improve Your Software Development*, offer something specific like, *10 Tools to Increase Your Development Team's Productivity by 30%.*

Entry Point Offer

Your entry point offer – or EPO – is an impulse buy that makes it easy for your prospects to become customers.

Jason Swenk from JasonSwenk.com, an expert in helping agencies and consulting companies improve their marketing, describes the EPO as a "foot in the door" offer. Instead of trying to sell your core service, which can be a large web design project, software development project, or a monthly retainer, sell them something small, instead.

Swenk says the "foot in the door" offer is a small taste of what it's like to work with you. It's something that's easy to sell, because it's priced low enough that the person you're talking to does not have to go to the CFO to get approval for a budget.

According to Swenk, a customer is 20 times more likely to purchase your core offering after they've bought your "foot in the door" EPO than if you had tried to sell them your core offering right away.

Swenk lists a few examples of "foot in the door" EPOs, as follows:

A Discovery

A discovery is where you schedule a half-day or full day session with your customer to explore their business. Your goal is to find hidden problems you can help them with. The deliverable is a report listing all the opportunities for improvement your customer has. They can either choose to hire you to solve these issues, or go to a competitor to get them resolved.

A Roadmapping Session

Web development agency Rootstrap.com uses roadmapping before starting any mobile app development project. In fact, their "rootstrapping" process (their proprietary name for roadmapping) has catapulted them into one of the top web development agencies in the U.S.

These sessions are typically a three-week discovery and planning session for which they charge $15,000. The end-result is a working proof-of-concept that startups have used to raise millions of dollars in venture funding. Roadmapping sessions are a great way to plan a development project.

But, more importantly, it's a way to charge your customers for the discovery and planning most consulting companies typically do for free before writing a full proposal for their core services. Brennan Dunn of DoubleYourFreelanceBusiness.com, and Ben Lee, co-founder and director of Roostrap.com, teach a course on how to sell roadmapping sessions.

An Audit

When Swenk was running his agency (before he sold it) he used to sell a lot of audits. He offered PPC optimization services, and the audits were designed to discover how much money the customers were losing on inefficient or wasted PPC campaigns. After the audit, he delivered a report that showed clients exactly how much money he could save them. The costs typically ran into the thousands per month.

Proof of Concepts

Many companies offer free functional proofs of concept of applications using HTML5. They look and behave just like real apps, except they're not connected to any data sources. I believe it's better to charge for a proof of concept instead of offering it for free. It's a more effective way of triggering the *commitment and consistency* factor in your customer's mind. It turns them into an actual customer, making them want to be consistent with that new status and want to continue being your customer.

Your Core Offering

The lead magnet and the EPO all lead up to one thing: positioning yourself to sell your core offering. If you've been able to sell an EPO, then asking your client to purchase your core offering is a logical next step for your customer. It's just like asking your significant other to marry you after you've introduced the parents.

The fact they purchased your audit, roadmapping session, or discovery means they are interested in the result your core offering can bring them.

But you must decide what your core offering is. Is it a one-time project, or is it a retainer? I would like to suggest that your core offering should be a one-time project, and that a monthly retainer is a *profit maximizer.* I describe the profit maximizer below.

When do you make the core offering? Typically, after you've finished delivering your EPO, or "foot in the door" project. The deliverables from an audit, discovery, or roadmapping session should map out next steps for your customers. The next steps are your core offering.

Swenk positions a one-time project as the next logical step. This can be an app development project, a new website, or something else that has a finite deliverable and schedule.

The Profit Maximizer

Ryan Deiss says that often a core offering is still not the vehicle that makes your company profitable. He cites the example of McDonald's, which is known as a fast food hamburger restaurant. McDonald's markets hamburgers, but when you walk into the restaurant they offer fries and a soda, as well – a value meal. McDonald's pioneered the concept of the value meal. For a fixed price you get the hamburger, fries, and a drink.

McDonald's makes its profit on the meal, not on the hamburger. But the hamburger is the core offering. For McDonald's, the cost of acquiring a single customer is $1.91, and the cost of a hamburger is $2.09. They make only $0.18 profit – which is almost no profit. But McDonald's makes $1.14 extra when it sells fries and a drink along with that hamburger. That's $1.32 profit per customer!

A typical profit maximizer for a consulting company is a retainer deal. By charging from $5,000 to $20,000 per month or more, you boost the profits you make on each customer, plus you generate steady cash flow that is vital to your company.

What additional services could you offer that can serve

as profit maximizers? If your core offer is staff augmentation services, maybe your profit maximizer could be turnkey project software development that you manage. If your core offer is outsourced customer service, maybe your profit maximizer could be sales qualification services. If your core offer is SAP integration services, maybe your profit maximizer could be big data services.

The Return Path

Finally, what are you going to do to get your customers to return to you more often to buy more products or services? If you offer retainer services, that's not a problem. However, if you only do project work, you need a way to keep your customers coming back for more – and coming back more frequently.

That's where customer marketing comes in. Marketing does not end when you acquire a new customer. That's when it begins.

You need to offer additional marketing communications strategies to keep your company top of mind with your customers. The best way to do that is good old-fashioned email. Send out regular emails that provide education, information about special deals your company is running, or inviting your customers to webinars, events, or conferences.

8

CONCLUSION

We've come a long way. In Chapter 1, we discussed the need for you to sell a transformation instead of talking about your service. You need to talk about how you can take your customers from a dissatisfied "before" state to a transformational "after" state.

Then, in Chapter 2, we discussed how you need to turn your service into your best marketing tool, through customer-centricity, the culture of innovation, continuous optimization, and corporate agility. In this day and age of instant viral communications, bad news about a company's service can spread quickly and can literally sink a company. But, delivering fantastic service can also spread virally.

In Chapter 3 we discussed the need to produce authority content. Whether you publish a report on some piece of original research your company conducted, or you write a book, or you deliver a free three-part video course, you become a trusted authority in the eyes of your prospects and your marketplace. This increases the likelihood that prospects will answer your phone calls or choose you instead of a competitor.

In Chapter 4 we discussed how you need to completely change the purpose of your website. Instead of treating it like a virtual brochure, talking about your services, use the concept of the "app" to make your website functional and useful. Give your prospects something to do: download a lead magnet, educate themselves, schedule an appointment. Tell them how to do business with you. Get them to visualize what it's like to be your client.

In Chapter 5 we talked about the need to drive traffic to your website. Gone are the days of "if you build it, they will come." Driving traffic needs to be a purposeful, methodical act. You can use paid traffic, earned traffic, organic traffic, and owned traffic. The Holy Grail is owned traffic, and that means building a mailing list of prospects who are happy to receive your latest blog posts or podcasts in their inbox. Having owned traffic means you must think and act like a media company, in addition to whatever it is you do (software development, BPO, customer support, etc.).

In Chapter 6, we recognized that, despite living in a digital world, outbound sales and marketing is alive and well – especially when you have a limited market. There's no point in waiting for all 500 of your target customers to suddenly discover your website and contact you. You need to reach out to them. But do it in the modern, 21st century way. Execute *contact campaigns* as described in Stu Heinecke's book *How to Get a Meeting with Anyone.*

Finally, in Chapter 7 we brought it all together and discussed how to actually sell your services. Most companies get this part completely wrong. They try to sell their core services right off the bat. It's like they're asking someone to marry them just two hours after meeting them at a party. We proposed the *escalation method* as way to ease your customers into the relationship, so that each step along the way is a logical, natural next step for your customers.

Your Next Steps

The steps I outline in this book can seem overwhelming, and I'm sure you're asking yourself, "Where do I start?"

Start with Chapter 7, how to sell your actual service. You need to create the exact flow that will get customers into a relationship with you that escalates into a full-blown engagement. Think about how you can get them into that *commitment and consistency* mindset by offering a small initial commitment, the lead magnet. Then an EPO, the impulse buy. And, finally, your core offering and your profit maximizers.

Reverse-engineer your sales process in your home country. If you're from Mexico, Argentina, Brazil, or Jamaica, how do you sell your services? Where does that conversation take place? How do you typically close the sale? What do you say to your prospects? What do they say to you? What happens right before the sale? Do you meet at a restaurant? Do you have several phone calls?

Really try to identify the exact details of that sales conversation. Identify any trends or patterns you've noticed that are common to all your most successful sales calls, then design an EPO and a lead magnet for the U.S. market that can replicate that sales scenario for you.

If you're just starting out, this doesn't have to be online at all. In fact, at the beginning it should be manual.

Find conferences in the U.S. that your prospective customers attend. Go to the conference and book a hotel suite near the conference (or at the conference hotel). Schedule an intimate executive briefing where you will teach an early version of your authority content. At this stage, your authority content will be just a PowerPoint presentation that you will deliver live.

Then contact as many event attendees as you can who fit the profile of your ideal customer. Invite them to your exclusive event, and offer to serve food and drinks. You should have no more than six or eight executives attend. Make sure these are top executives, like Directors of Development, CIOs, or something similar.

Deliver the presentation as a true, educational event. Don't turn this into a glorified sales call – you'll just turn everybody off. Offer something of value, like "How to Digitally Transform Your Company on a Budget," or something like that.

A week before the conference follow-up with the confirmed attendees and ask them for their biggest concern related to the topic. Ask them, "What is the single biggest challenge you're struggling with in your business, right now?"

This will help you to customize the presentation to your audience so that you answer their questions, making you more relevant and increasing the chances you can obtain your first clients.

Finally, after you deliver your executive briefing in an educational format, *then* you can announce that you're offering a special deal for a limited time. This is when you introduce your audit, roadmapping session, or some other low-cost entry point offer.

About Content Marketing Latam

Content Marketing Latam provides education and consulting services for Latin American companies who want to implement content-based digital marketing strategies to expand their market and sell more. Through our consulting division, Nearshore Marketing, we specialize in helping outsourcing companies with their U.S. digital marketing strategies.

If you'd like us to help you with the strategies described here, contact us at fernando@contentmarketinglatam.com, or call me at +1 512-945-9273. We will schedule an initial 20-minute strategy session and determine if you're ready to work with us. You can also visit us at https://contentmarketinglatam.com and http://nearshoremarketing.com

The next step would be to schedule a one-day, onsite strategy session to map out your U.S. marketing strategy. After the workshop, we will deliver a full strategy and roadmap with timelines and KPIs that you can either use to implement yourself, or hire us to execute for you.

ABOUT THE AUTHOR

About Fernando Labastida

Content marketer Fernando Labastida was a pioneer in the content marketing scene, having founded the Austin Content Marketing meetup, and launching the first Spanish-language content marketing blog for the Latin American market.

Fernando is also the founder of Content Marketing LatAm, Latin America's premiere educational resource for content marketing education. He is also the founder of Nearshore Marketing and Content Propulsion.

He writes for the Content Marketing Institute, Relevance and AGBeat, and has spoken at SXSW, the Niche Digital Conference in Chicago, the Content Marketing Summit and Mobile Marketing Summit in Mexico, and the CIES Social Media Summit in El Salvador. He has helped B2B technology companies, from large to small by executing bold content marketing initiatives.